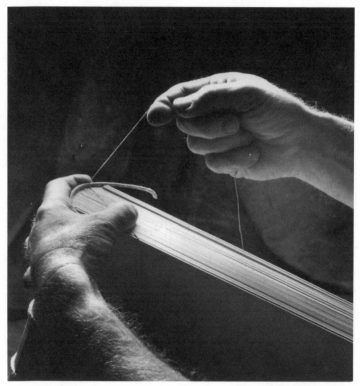

Photograph by Jon Van Allen

A DEGREE OF MASTERY

A Journey through Book Arts Apprenticeship

ANNIE TREMMEL WILCOX

Minnesota Voices Project Number 88
New Rivers Press 1999

New Rivers Press is a nonprofit literary press dedicated to publishing the very
best emerging writers in our region, nation, and world.

The quotations on pages 52, 54, 58, 60, 68, 70, 75, and 77 are excerpted with
permission from *Japanese Woodworking Tools: Their Tradition, Spirit and Use*
by Toshio Ōdate. © 1984 by The Taunton Press, Inc. All rights reserved.

Epigraph quotation is printed with permission from *Simple Cooking*, a quarterly
food newsletter (no. 25, 1989, p. 6) by John Thorne. © 1989 by John Thorne.

The publication of *A Degree of Mastery* has been made possible by generous
grants from the Jerome Foundation; the North Dakota Council on the Arts; and
Target Stores, Dayton's, and Mervyn's by the Dayton Hudson Foundation.

This activity is made possible in part by a grant provided by the Minnesota
State Arts Board, through an appropriation by the Minnesota State Legislature.
In addition, this activity is supported in part by a grant from the National
Endowment for the Arts.

Additional support has been provided by the General Mills Foundation, the
McKnight Foundation, the Star Tribune Foundation, and the contributing
members of New Rivers Press.

New Rivers Press
420 North Fifth Street
Minneapolis, MN 55401

www.mtn.org/newrivpr

To Timothy Barrett, Don Guyot, Kim Merker,
and Paul Diehl, teachers who have guided and
inspired me on this journey. To Scot, Zachary,
and Emily, and our families.

And to the memory of William Anthony,
master bookbinder.

*The difference between the simple knowledge
of a craft and its mastery is the difference between
ingestion...and a period of digestion.*

—John Thorne, *Simple Cooking*

CONTENTS

Acknowledgments

ACKNOWLEDGMENTS

I would like to thank Paul Diehl, Kim Merker, Tom Simmons, Dennis Moore, Carol Severino, Jim Downey, Pat Miller, Emily Martin, and Janice Frey, who offered suggestions and encouragement as the writing and revision of this work progressed. Bill Truesdale and the staff of New Rivers Press, Jim Cihlar, Phyllis Jendro, Jennifer Song, Mary Byers, and Nordis Heyerdahl-Fowler provided great insight and support.

My thanks are due to staff at the University of Iowa's Main Library, David Schoonover, Susan Hanson, Judy Macy, Barbara Dewey, and Margaret Richardson, who helped me retrieve information about library exhibitions, Bill Anthony's early work for the university, the acquisition of the Chef Louis Szathmary Culinary Arts Collection, Special Collections' holdings, and the ceremony restoring the Iowa State Constitution to the state. Pam Spitzmueller guided me through a number of the processes described in the treatment of *A Circumstantial Narrative of the Campaign in Russia* in the first chapter.

Thanks also go to Kim Merker, University of Iowa Center for the Book, who gave me access to archival material pertaining to Bill Anthony's position at the university; and to Jane Meggers, State Historical Society of Iowa, for providing information on the initial attempt to restore the constitution.

Many thanks are due to Jon Van Allen, who took the photograph of Bill Anthony's hands, and for permission for me to use the photograph here. Special thanks also go to Cheryl Jacobsen, whose delicate line drawings capture the heart of the bookbinding tools they depict.

I would also like to thank Larry Yerkes, Sally Key, Jane Meggers, Jim Downey, Penny McKean, and Lisa Anthony, who worked with me during my apprenticeship with Bill Anthony.

Most of all, I would like to thank my husband, Scot, for his great love, support, encouragement, and child care while I wrote this. And for letting me buy all those tools.

BEGINNINGS
AND ENDINGS

Glue brush

A Circumstantial Narrative of the Campaign in Russia. This book has come downstairs to my workbench in Conservation from Special Collections because it needs treatment. It's not old—it was printed in 1817—and will be a good book for me to practice conservation techniques with. I pull out a treatment survey and report sheet and begin to fill it out.

This book's major problem is that it doesn't have any covers. All that remains attached to the text block is the original leather spine of the binding with its label. The leather appears to be calf and has red rot, a condition of older leather that causes it to turn red and crumble at the slightest touch. As I examine it, the spine leaves leather smudges all over my hands. Since this is a tight-back book where the leather cover is glued directly to the back of the text block, I will probably not be able to save the spine piece. With luck, however, I will be able to remove and reuse the label.

Next I begin to examine the text block. As I open it, I notice the faint musty smell older books often have. I can see that the pages are foxed (spotted with rust from bits of iron in the paper there as a result of the way the paper was made or sized). I will probably be able to lighten the stains as I treat the paper but not remove them. Foxing this bad usually doesn't come out in the wash.

I page through the text block carefully. Facing the title page is a frontispiece—the stereotypical picture of Napoleon, lock of hair over his forehead, hand in his coat front. The foxing is worse on these two pages, and as a result Napoleon has a very ruddy complexion. The rust stains continue throughout the rest of the book. The edges of the pages are ragged in places, and the frontispiece has a tear that extends from the fore edge of the page down through Napoleon's portrait and goes just past his left ear and into his shoulder.

The other major problem with *Campaign* is that the paper of the text block is very soft. The edges of the pages are slightly ruffled and torn in places. Whatever internal or external sizing this paper may have will wash away, leaving these pages even softer and more vulnerable. This will be a problem. I will probably have to resize the paper to strengthen it before I reassemble the text block. One of the primary things my job as a book and paper conservator entails is leaving an item in better condition than it was when I received it.

I complete the survey sheet, noting everything I can about *Campaign* and its condition. Not only will this serve as my record of the treatment, but a copy will stay here in the Conservation Department to answer any questions someone may have later about the condition of this book before treatment. Then I take a set of documentation slides that show the book's lack of covers, its spine, the title page and frontispiece of

Napoleon, and sample interior pages. Once I have finished treating the book, I will take another set of slides to show how it's been improved. I take a pencil and letter the pages that aren't numbered, mostly front matter, so that I can get the pages back in the correct order later. The graphite won't hurt the book or come off during treatment.

Now I am ready to begin "pulling" the text block—the process of taking it apart for treatment. I open a tool drawer and take out my lifting knife.

○ ○ ○

It was a sunny day in October 1983 the first time I met Bill Anthony. I was busy setting type at Windhover Press, the University of Iowa's letterpress, where I was a student of Kim Merker's. I had been working there for three years, slowly learning all that goes into the letterpress printing of fine books. I liked the rhythm of setting type by hand and pulling freshly printed sheets of text. Eventually I hoped to become Kim's assistant at the press. I was the only person working in the shop that afternoon when he asked if I would like to go over to the health sciences library with him. A bookbinder and conservator from Chicago named Bill Anthony was bringing back some of the books he had worked on for the library's John Martin Rare Book Room. Anthony was going to show slides of the treatments he'd performed, and Kim wanted to see them.

I had been in the health sciences library before, but never in the rare book room. It's stuck in an out-of-the-way corner on the second floor. When we arrived, a few other people were milling about looking at the books in the display cases. Kim knew who they were and went to talk to them. As I looked at the books, I noticed I was the only woman in the room. A slide projector was set up on one of the long tables. After a few minutes people began taking seats. I sat down next to Kim just as the lights were dimmed.

The first slide was a before-treatment picture of a Vesalius, a mid-seventeenth-century medical book, that appeared to be in bad shape. The pages looked dirty and broken in places—not a book that could be handled easily. My attention was drawn, however, away from the slide to the man narrating. He appeared to be in his midfifties, a gentle man with a serious face and a soft voice. It was the voice that caught me with its strong hint of Ireland. This was Bill Anthony.

I was fascinated as he continued through the slides. He had taken this book completely apart to treat it. I was only familiar with putting together new books. How did he get the pages apart? How was it possible to wash and dry a book? How did he ever get all the pages together again, in the right order, and bound? I was enthralled. One man off to the side kept asking questions. When the slide show was over and Kim introduced me to people, I was to discover that this was Dr. John Martin, the man who had donated a large number of valuable and rare historical medical books to the university and the man for whom this room was named. He had come all the way from Clarinda, Iowa, to see how Bill Anthony had treated his books. The Vesalius had been one of the jewels of his collection.

The last slide showed the book, now rebound and covered in alum-tawed pigskin, a rich white leather, with tooled lines that crisscrossed in a diamond pattern on the cover. When the lights came up, the book was on a table in the front of the room. It seemed like magic that this book was now restored to a condition where people could pick it up and easily turn the pages without harming it. Dr. Martin and the others examined the Vesalius while Kim introduced me to Mr. Anthony, who warmly shook my hand. He had red hair, now going to gray, and wore khaki pants and a blue oxford shirt with the sleeves rolled up to the elbows. He smiled and patted Kim on the back as he shook his hand.

I had just managed to tell him how much I enjoyed seeing his slides when Dr. Martin came up with the Vesalius to ask some more questions. Kim and I left, and on the way back to the press, he told me Bill Anthony was thinking of closing his business in Chicago. Kim was trying to convince the university that Bill should come to Iowa and begin a conservation department in the Main Library. Maybe Bill would even teach bookbinding classes.

Kim knew I was interested in bookbinding as a sideline to printing because I was working a couple of afternoons a week for the local binder of the Windhover Press books. In the afternoons when I worked at the press setting type, Kim would often tell me about the Center for the Book he was scheming to create at Iowa. Having a bookbinder-conservator around sounded like a good plan. He had an idea about a young papermaker who might like to come and teach at the university too. I had liked Mr. Anthony and was amazed that he could successfully take books apart and put them back together again in better condition. I had no idea that there were people who did this sort of thing.

○ ○ ○

As I suspected, the spine leather is so rotted it comes easily away from where it is glued to the back of the text block. I slide the edge of the lifting knife under one side of the leather and slice the spine off in crumbling strips. Carefully, I remove the leather label in one piece. I'll clean the back of the rotted leather later. For now I place it in a labeled envelope so that it won't get mislaid.

Once I slice and scrape the rest of the leather off the back of the book, I must remove the animal-hide glue that holds the spine lining material on and the backs of the sections together. It has dried hard, resembling the mucilage glue I had used as a child in school. When this glue is removed the book will come apart more easily.

The book is already in the job backer, a large iron standing press that clamps the text block firmly so that the spine is facing up and can be worked on. I prepare a dry paste about the consistency of Cream of Wheat that has sat too long and heap it in mounds all along the spine's surface. The paste allows moisture to slowly soften the lining and glue so that they can be scraped off. The book must sit for half an hour, so I drape a piece of Saran Wrap over the paste to keep it from drying out too quickly.

Later I remove the Saran Wrap and scrape the paste off the back of the book carefully with my bone folder—a long, slender, polished piece of bone reminiscent of a tongue depressor. The mull, an open-mesh, starched fabric that was glued onto *Campaign* as a spine lining, is soft now and peels up from the backs of the sections. Next I take the pointed end of my bone folder and scrape the brown animal-hide glue off the backs of the sections of paper that make up this book. It comes off in most places, but another application of wheat paste is needed before it comes off completely. Moisture has softened the back of the sections, and I have to be careful not to scrape away any of the paper.

Quickly I take the book out of the job backer and put it on my workbench. I have to pull the text before the backs of the sections dry out again. I reach into one of my tool drawers and take out a pair of curved dissecting scissors and a pair of hemostats, the delicate gripping tools used by surgeons. I open the text block to the very center of the first section where the threads of sewing show. Lifting them up just a bit with the hemostats, I clip the threads with the scissors. Then

I close the section again and, grabbing it gently by the fore edge of the pages, pull it away from the rest of the text block. If there is any glue left along the spine of the section, the sections will still come away because it is damp and soft. I continue to do this for the rest of the text block. If I tried to pull the book dry, I would tear off the backs of the sections, making more repair work for myself later. Since *Campaign* is so thick, I have to continually redampen the spine of the sections with a large, wet cotton swab.

Now that the sections have been pulled, it's time to wash the book. I get out several white photographic trays that are large enough to hold the sections of *Campaign* when they are opened flat into folios—sheets folded once in the middle. I also get out a stack of wet-strength paper that is cut to fit these trays. This paper is used to support pages during washing and deacidification. It is almost impossible to handle wet sheets of paper without tearing them. Ordinary paper loses eighty percent of its strength when it's wet. Wet-strength paper holds up because it's impregnated with a resin that coats the fibers and keeps it strong in water.

Since there is so much foxing and staining on the pages of *Campaign,* I half fill one of the trays with heated deionized water out of a sterling silver tap resistant to the water's corrosive powers on metal. Warm water floats more impurities out of the paper than cold. I submerge one piece of wet-strength paper and follow by submerging two folios of *Campaign* on top, watching to make sure the paper wets out completely. The old book smell suddenly becomes much more pungent. I continue alternating wet-strength paper with folios of the text, adding more water to the tray as necessary. The whole book takes up two trays.

By the time I have finished with the second tray, the water in the first is bright yellow with the impurities that have washed out of the paper. I drain off this water and add fresh, repeating this process over the course of several hours until the water ceases to turn yellow, changing the water in the trays every half hour. Now it is time to deacidify the paper.

○ ○ ○

Kim's dream for the Center for the Book began to materialize, and in the spring of 1985, I was among the students in the first bookbinding class Bill Anthony taught after setting up the Conservation Department in the university's Main Library. My work with Kim at Windhover Press had led me to a job at a local edition bindery, and I was thrilled to have a chance to move beyond the simple types of bindings I did there to study with Bill. He had seemed very nice when I had gone to get his signature on my registration sheet. He asked polite questions about the job I'd had at the bindery.

The class met on Wednesday nights for two and a half hours in a makeshift book arts room in the Art Building. We had book presses and workbenches, but no paper cutter. Bill had to bring materials to class precut. He had planned several bindings for us to do, and each class began with a demonstration of the steps we would do that evening. Then, as we worked, Bill moved among us answering questions and helping with any problems we had. It was a tight squeeze, and my first impression was that he was genial and easy to work with, although the lack of a paper cutter obviously bothered him.

The class was an odd mix of students. There were two schoolteachers with fancy manicures and clean work aprons. There was Tom, the only male in the class, who soon became one of Bill's racquetball partners. And there was Nadine. She was a graduate student in the Math Department who was good with numbers, but not with her hands. She also took everything Bill said literally.

For example, the first night of class Bill showed slides of a conservation treatment. The slide projected on the wall depicted pages of a book washing in a tray of water. Nadine asked if the spin cycle of the washer didn't damage the pages of the book. And what about the dryer? I knew from having been at various book arts lectures with her that Nadine had a habit of asking serious questions that seemed to show a complete lack of common sense. It was a while before Bill learned to ignore her and just go on with his explanations. Never before had he taught a class where he hadn't handpicked the students from a pool of interested binders.

And there was Greta. She worked with me at Windhover, filling book orders and keeping track of who owed what. Expecting her first child, she grew in size as the semester progressed. One night as she was putting a book in the nipping press, Greta turned the handle the wrong way so that the platen of the press flew up instead of clamping down on her book. Bill was standing next to her, watching.

"That's the problem with women," he said to Greta, watching the platen go down toward the book as she spun the handle the other way. "They can never screw right."

Greta looked down at her expanding waistline and back up at him and replied, "Oh, I don't know. I think I've proved that I'm pretty good at screwing." Fair-skinned Bill turned a deep crimson and laughed.

I had no idea at the time that this gentle man with his sly sense of humor was one of the most famous book conservators and binders in the country. He and his apprentices in his shop in Chicago had bound editions for the foremost printers in the United States. His fine, one-of-a-kind leather bindings sold for thousands of dollars. He conserved rare and valuable books for libraries throughout the Chicago area and beyond. Books like the giant folio editions of Audubon's *Birds of America*. I knew none of this. At this point he was just another teacher, although he was one I liked and respected very much.

One evening we were learning the Coptic, a four-needle stitch that has been used to bind Egyptian books since the second century. Bill had explained the sewing pattern to the class and was facing me over the workbench, trying to guide me through it. Nadine was sitting next to me trying to thread one of her needles.

Bill, finally frustrated at my botched sewing of the sections of the book, came over and made me get up so that he could show me how to do it. He took up the slightly curved needles and began sewing the next section of paper to the text block. But he got mixed up at the point where the needles passed each other, changing sewing directions, and had to take the stitches out and start over again. At this point I leaned over and asked, "Are you sure you've done this before?"

Again he turned crimson. Then he laughed and replied, "I think so." He got the sewing started again, showed me how to attach the section correctly, and I took my place at the workbench to finish sewing the text block. Nadine was still threading her needles.

◊ ◊ ◊

I stand the photographic trays up in the big sink to drain off the deionized wash water from the folios of *Campaign*. After half an hour, I lay the trays back down and pour a solution of magnesium bicarbonate into them. We prepare this buffer ourselves by bubbling carbon dioxide through two large glass containers of magnesium carbonate powder mixed with deionized water, siphoning out the resulting solution into plastic jugs. Once in the trays, the buffer is adjusted with the addition of more deionized water until the pH is around 8, indicating that the solution is alkaline. The folios soak in the magnesium bicarbonate between the sheets of wet-strength tissue for about half an hour.

This is one of the standard procedures for buffering paper. Through washing, I have removed as many soluble acids as possible, and this next bath will deposit a buffer in the paper that I hope will neutralize any acids that remain in the sheets. Although it is possible to age paper artificially and see how well it lasts after being treated this way, conservation science is still too new to know how well such treatments will endure over the years.

After half an hour, I stand the trays up again and drain off the magnesium bicarbonate solution. I carefully place the sets of wet-strength, each with two folios of the text trapped between them, on the drying racks to air-dry overnight. The next morning, I remove the papers from the drying racks, peel apart the sets, and separate the folios from the wet-strength paper. It amazes me to see how little the sheets have cockled in the drying process. Because this paper is so soft, the slight tear across Napoleon's portrait has lengthened during handling. Other edge tears will also need repair. But the pages are noticeably cleaner and less stained and spotted after treatment.

I can feel how much softer the pages have become as a result of being washed and buffered. The sizing in the paper, put in originally to protect and strengthen it like spray starch on shirts, contributed greatly to the yellow color of the wash water and is almost completely gone. I could go ahead and mend the sheets and rebind the book, but the pages would be more susceptible to dirt and tears if left this way. It will be better if I resize them first.

I make the solution for resizing by mixing a third of a cup of Methocel 4AC into hot water. The fine white methyl cellulose powder disperses in hot water but does not dissolve. I then add a cup of room-temperature deionized water and the mixture begins to thicken. Adding another cup of cold deionized water from the refrigerator causes the Methocel to thicken more into a smooth solution not unlike runny Jell-O. This is the magic powder that is sold by the ton to McDonald's to keep their shakes thick. I thin mine out a little more until it's runny, but still a bit slimy to the touch, and pour it into one of the trays.

I place each folio of *Campaign* between two sheets of Hollytex, a thin sheet of spun polyester, and submerge it into the Methocel. The Hollytex has an open texture, and the liquid passes through it easily. Yet it is strong enough to support the weight of the wet, resized sheet as I lift it out of the solution and lay it to drain on a slanted sheet of Plexiglas in the sink. I blot each folio to remove excess moisture, carefully transfer it to dry sheets of Hollytex, and place it back on the drying rack. To do this for more than two hundred pages of text takes a very long time. Several days, in fact, because I can only lay out a dozen sets of folios on the drying racks at once.

As the sheets are finished, I carefully refold them into sections following the pagination and my own penciled notations. I layer the sections between pieces of binder's board and weight them gently over several days, gradually pressing out what slight cockling has occurred as a result of resizing, but not pressing out the impression made by the type when the pages were printed. Next the tears will be mended.

○ ○ ○

During that first semester I studied with Bill, I began to feel a companionship with him I had never known with any other teacher. He had a deep love for his work that I found contagious. He was always enthusiastic. He always listened to his students when we spoke to him. Even Nadine was a valued and important member of the class, no matter how far from common sense she strayed. For me, it was like being in a room with a chocolate cake: I always wanted more. Late that spring I also discovered the great talent of this craftsman.

In February, Bill had mounted an exhibit of bindings in the University of Iowa Museum of Art, *The Art and Craft of Bookbinding.* One class night in April just before the exhibit was to come down, he arranged for a museum guard to let us see the exhibit after hours. As we waited on the steps of the museum to be let in, I had no idea what to expect. Other than the work Bill had demonstrated in class, I had only seen the Vesalius he had treated for the health sciences library. I had no idea what other types of work he did. The binder I had worked for took letterpress editions and put them into plain paper and cloth covers a lot like what you find under the dust jackets of hardcovers in the bookstore. I was about to be enlightened.

A guard wearing a gun met us at the door and let us in the museum, showing us where to hang up our coats and backpacks. Lighting was low except in a small gallery up the stairs to the right as we went in. Bill handed each of us a glossy exhibit brochure containing a brief history of bookbinding and told us to look around and let him know if we had any questions. Freestanding cases throughout the room were filled with books of designs and styles that I could never have imagined. I walked from one Plexiglas-covered case to another in a state of openmouthed amazement.

There were conservation treatments Bill had done for the library. A fourteenth-century manuscript written on vellum had been rebound in a warm honey-brown leather with windowpane lines tooled into the covers. I wanted to pick it up and open the small brass clasps holding it shut to see the pages inside. Another one of Bill's bindings was a German book from 1687 bound in vellum with intricate lettering on its wide spine. It was held closed by tiny pegs resembling small bone folders slipped through alum-tawed pigskin thongs. A big book, it looked quite light in its vellum cover. I wanted to open it and see how the vellum cover moved in my hands.

There were cases and cases of French and English "fine bindings." Bill explained to us that these were books decorated more artistically than the conservation bindings— usually in colored leathers with designs of leather inlaid and edged with gold tooling. Many were on loan from Dr. Samuel Rosenthal, a friend of Bill's from Chicago. A number of the fine bindings had been done by Bill.

I was transfixed in front of a case containing a large book by Bill covered in bright green leather. On its cover were onlaid strips of bright red leather that formed a rectangle with a diamond interwoven with it. These were framed by two larger red leather-strip rectangles. Everywhere the red and the green met was a perfectly straight line of gold tooling. The colors were more vivid than any I had ever seen before on a book cover. I looked up to see Bill standing on the other side of the case, looking at me with amusement.

"How did you do this?" I asked him. "How did you keep the gold line so straight?" As he proceeded with an explanation involving gold foil and things called "rolls" and "pieces of line," I knew that whatever the process, I wanted to learn how to do it. I wanted to be this man's student until I knew how to make books as beautiful as these. I wanted the whole chocolate cake.

So I continued to take Bill's class. In the fall of 1985, he moved us from the Art Building to the Conservation Department in the Main Library so that we could have access to the equipment we needed. There were some new students (we had lost the two tidy schoolteachers—but the rest of the class remained). Bill decided to have everyone do the same initial project, and then let us each choose what we wanted to do after that.

We started out by making three small quarter-cloth bindings with marbled paper on the front and back covers. None of us had ever done any case binding, which, unlike the non-adhesive bindings we had done the semester before, required using adhesives. We learned quickly that it was a bit tricky to keep the glue only where we wanted it. I enjoyed making these three books, all exactly the same except for the different marbled papers I used on their covers.

Bill had given us free rein over the materials in the department, and I was often paralyzed by the choices. I spent most of one evening just leafing through the two drawers of marbled papers, each sheet carefully decorated by hand. They were the most beautiful sheets of paper I had ever seen. Bill finally came over and teased me about taking so long to make up my mind, even though I was still ahead of almost everyone else in getting my books completed. I was to learn later he didn't much care for marbled papers and almost never used them on his own bindings. He generously bought these for his students to use. Some of them had been given to him by former students and friends who made marbled papers.

I responded to his teasing by picking out three of the brightest and wildest papers I could find. The first had fine veins of teal blue, brown, and two shades of bright orange. The second had a fine feathery pattern in glowing turquoise and green. And the third was scalloped in purple, sky blue, and white. But they were all made on base sheets of dark cream that almost matched perfectly the cloth I chose for the spines. My books turned out well and felt nice in my hands. And the colors made Bill wince noticeably. Many years later, I discovered that these vivid papers were marbled by Norma Rubovits, one of America's foremost paper marblers and a former binding student of Bill's in Chicago.

By the time the semester was over I was hooked. The previous summer, I had quit working for the edition binder in town who did the Windhover books. I had definitely decided that doing one or two similar bindings was much more agreeable than doing two hundred and fifty exactly alike. I liked Bill's approach to his work. He was meticulous and didn't panic when things didn't go right with our books. He simply helped us correct them, calmly and carefully. He said that there was no mistake in binding that you couldn't correct or redo, and I found that comforting.

○ ○ ○

Paper mending can be a tedious and time-consuming process. I am lucky in this case. The tears in *Campaign* are along the edges of the pages and, with the exception of Napoleon's portrait, will go quickly. The principle is simple: a tear in paper is stabilized by gluing another piece of paper to it—just like adhesive tape, only better. I lay out the tools and supplies I will need on the top of my bench and prepare my adhesive.

Every conservator I talk to has different opinions about adhesives. Some use pure starch paste—derived from flours with the proteins and glutens removed—for their work. Some use "mix"—pastes combined with other adhesives such as PVA (polyvinyl acetate—a kissing cousin of Elmer's glue) or methyl cellulose. Others use rabbit or fish glues. The choice of adhesive depends on a number of things, but, for most, the ideal is to use the purest adhesive in the weakest strength that will accomplish a specific task. Adhesives applied in conservation are supposed to be reversible, so that if for any reason they need to be removed later, they can be.

For mending *Campaign* I will use *ʒin shofu*, a Japanese wheat-starch paste. I measure a third of a cup of the thin off-white powder and mix it with three cups of deionized water to soak for twenty minutes before it is cooked. Conservators used to spend the cooking time stirring the paste in a saucepan over a hot plate. Now the mixture is put into the nonstick saucepan of a Cook'n'Stir, the type of kitchen appliance used to make hollandaise sauce. It has a heating element with temperature control and a rotating blade that stirs continuously. Once the *ʒin shofu* sits for twenty minutes, I simply turn on the machine, and it stirs and cooks the paste for me.

Twenty minutes later the opaque white mixture has thickened considerably and turned translucent. I remove it from the pan, sieve it while adding deionized water to thin it to the consistency of smooth gravy, and pour it into a plastic container that has been sprayed on the inside with Lysol to retard spoilage and the growth of mold. I spoon paste into a small clear glass bowl and thin it further with water until it is almost runny.

While the paste cooks, I lay out the tools I need for mending on my bench: a piece of clear, thin Mylar, several brushes, the bowl of paste, another bowl of deionized water, some tweezers, large cotton swabs, and an assortment of mending papers made from kozo, a long-fibered plant resembling bamboo that produces a tough yet thin paper. I also prepare a corner of my bench with strips of heavy blotter and Hollytex and weights.

I decide to begin with the frontispiece of Napoleon and do the difficult mend first. It is a jagged tear, but it has not warped during drying. The edges also meet all along their length, so there will be no gaps. If both sides of a tear don't meet evenly, the resulting gap must be filled in with kozo because pulling them together would cause warping elsewhere in the sheet. I turn the page over to do my primary mend from the back.

I wet-tear a strip of kozo three-eighths of an inch wide from a sheet similar in color to the text paper. This is done by running a thin lining brush full of water down the length of the kozo and pulling the narrow strip away. Because the kozo paper is made of long fibers, the tear is furry, resembling a thin paper centipede. I put the frontispiece under the sheet of Mylar and position the strip on top so that I can check how well it adheres to the contours of the tear. This tear is fairly straight; for crooked tears, the kozo can be wet-torn to match its configuration. I pull the page back out, and, leaving the mend strip on the Mylar, I paint it with the thin paste, making sure that my strokes pull the fibers out at right angles to the strip. I pull the kozo off the Mylar with the tweezers and lay it on the mend, carefully rolling it down with a large cotton swab that applies pressure and helps soak up extra moisture. Slowly, I make sure the two edges of the tear match. Long tears are usually mended in sections. I quickly sandwich the mend in between two pieces of Hollytex and two pieces of blotter, and weight till dry. Drying the mend under tension like this keeps it from cockling from the moisture I have introduced into a small area of the page. While this first tear dries, I do another, smaller edge tear in another page. Soon I have several mends drying on the corner of my bench.

I go back and check the frontispiece. The mend has dried flat and looks good from the back. I turn it over. The two portions of Napoleon are now rejoined. But just by handling the page I can tell that it has a tendency to bend along the tear line, so I need to reinforce it from the front as well. I attach another kozo strip across the front margin of the page and dry it. But I can't run a kozo mend across the portrait of Napoleon (the kozo mend will dry an opaque off-white and will obscure the fine black lines of the illustration). I tease another strip of kozo into a much smaller piece, spider shaped, that I can use to tack the tear at a point where I won't interfere with the illustration. I use the white space of Napoleon's epaulet. I have heard of conservators mending important texts with single kozo fibers so as not to obscure the printing, but fortunately Napoleon doesn't command such attention.

The page is stable when I have finished and will turn without buckling when the book is rebound. But the staining on the portrait side of the paper makes the kozo mends obvious. I touch them up lightly with colored pencils so that they blend in better. I don't want to hide the fact that the page has been mended, but I don't want my mends to distract from Napoleon either. The rest of the work goes quickly. I reassemble the folios into sections and order them into a text block. Finally, *Campaign* is ready to be resewn.

○ ○ ○

Bill and I had settled into a routine that fall semester. I was always the first one to class on Wednesday nights. I would wait in the hallway for Bill to come back to the library after having gone home for dinner. He would unlock the door, we would walk down the long corridor to Conservation, and talk about this and that. Books. Things I was working on at Windhover. What I was working on in class. He would show me what he was busy with at his bench. The rest of the students would drift in, and class would begin at seven.

At this point, after teaching the class for three semesters, Bill no longer assigned bindings that all the students were to do at the same time. Instead, each of us, after a chat with him, worked on whatever project we wanted to. Another school-teacher had joined the class, driving to Iowa City each week from Anamosa. She spent her time repairing her own books or books of friends. I was doing a sketchbook that would have a spine of leather (the first time I had worked with this material). Greta was making a book for the baby due mid-semester.

Bill would usually make a trip around the room, going from bench to bench as class began. He would answer any questions we had, and once everyone was busy working, he would go to his own bench and work on whatever project he had to do. Sometimes it was private commission work. Sometimes it was work for Special Collections. We knew that we could always interrupt him with any questions we had. Bill never made anyone feel like an intruder, and he gave his full attention to his answer, often putting down what he was doing to help a student at his or her bench.

When I came up behind him—his workbench faced the wall—I would always stop to see what he was doing before I asked my question. Often Bill would describe to me what he was doing and why. I was fascinated by his job and its privileges. To be able to handle rare and valuable books on a regular basis. To examine them and understand their structures.

That fall, Bill was working on the Petrus Comestor. This was a large book that had previously been rebound during the nineteenth century in a cloth-and-paper case binding. An incunabulum printed in 1473 during the earliest days of movable type, the Petrus was quite valuable. Bill had taken it out of its most recent binding and was rebinding it more appropriately. For several weeks, we watched the progression as

Bill dry-cleaned the pages, mended them, resewed the text block, and prepared to recover it.

For this new cover, Bill laced on huge oak boards, as the book measured roughly sixteen by eleven inches. From my studies of the history of printing and binding, I knew that books had once had wooden covers, but to actually see them placed on a book was impressive. Bill had sanded and stained the wood, fitting the boards to the shape and size of the text block. Watching him, I realized book conservation required knowledge of many things—including woodworking!

The next week during class, Bill was getting ready to put on a spine covering of leather that would extend over and cover a third of the front and back boards. He had ordered the leather from a woman in New York and showed it to us that night in class. It was goatskin, something Bill called "Super Chieftain." When he unrolled it, there was the unmistakable aroma of leather. He held up the supple skin and we could see from its shape that it had been an animal. In fact, it reminded me too vividly of some creature run over on the highway. But I liked the smell and feel of the skin, smooth and slightly knobby on one side and rough on the other, like the inside of one of my mother's leather handbags.

By the end of the semester, the binding was complete and Bill showed it to us one last time before it was boxed and returned to its home in Special Collections. The supple pages turned easily in their new binding. I could see that the first twenty pages still had some dirt and fingerprints on them that

Bill hadn't been able to remove. The first pages of a book are almost always the dirtiest since they get handled the most. I could see that the rubrication—the highlighting by hand in red—of each of the woodcut capital letters ended two-thirds of the way through the book. Obviously, the scribe had gone blind by that point. I stood and paged through the book with the others for quite some time. It was much better off in its new binding.

○ ○ ○

I fold new endsheets for *Campaign* and tip linen hinges to them with a thin stripe of adhesive. These hinges are strips of unbleached linen about an inch and a half wide and the length of the endsheets. They are creased lengthwise with the material on one side of the fold only one-sixteenth of an inch wide. The narrow sides are glued out and the hinges are adhered to the first and last sections, with the larger, unglued flaps of linen left free on the sides that will face the covers. These flaps will be adhered later to the inside of the covers, reinforcing the weakest area of the cover where the book swings open.

Now that the text block is complete, I can punch the holes in the folds of the sections and resew the book. There are already holes where the book was sewn previously. I use those and have to punch only three new holes in each section, using a thin card strip with notches cut in one edge. Each section is opened and placed fold down in a punching trough—

a V-shaped jig made out of wood. The card is placed down into the center of the section, and using the notches as guides, I punch through the section with my awl. Even though there are many sections to this book, punching holes this way doesn't take more than five minutes. Now the text block is ready for sewing.

This book consists of a number of thin sections. To keep down the swelling that could occur in the spine area due to too many lengths of sewing running back and forth through the sections, I am going to sew *Campaign* "two-on." I have never done this before, and just diagramming the sewing and getting it straight in my mind takes most of one morning. Unlike standard sewing, in which the thread runs up the length of one section and down the length of the next, I will weave in and out, running the length of thread up through two sections and down through two more. This was a technique first used in the nineteenth century to speed up book production in a era when all books were still sewn by hand. Binders found it much quicker to sew text blocks together two sections at a time.

I am going to sew this book on half-inch linen tapes and attach three of them to a sewing frame. This holds them taut at spaced intervals perpendicular to the text block, allowing me to sew up and back through the sections and weave the thread around these tapes for more stability. Later the tapes will be glued to the covering boards to help attach the text block securely.

I thread a needle with a thin linen thread, wax it so that it is less likely to knot, and begin to sew the sections. I follow the two-on diagram, making several false starts. Weaving up and back through two sections at a time is slow and confusing, and, although I can do it more quickly after sewing a third of the book, it takes me more than three hours to get all the sections sewn and to cut the tapes loose from the frame.

Next I must "forward" the text block—the steps done before the covers are attached. I return the book to the job backer, with the folded creases of the spine of the text block facing up. The tapes running across the back of the text block are held securely by the thin expanses of thread that run over them. I tighten the backer gently—just enough to hold the text block securely and keep it from falling through onto the floor. Then I glue up the spine of the text block with some of the *zin shofu* I used for mending. After a few minutes when it has dried, I apply a second layer of paste and a lining strip of the Japanese mending tissue—a slightly thicker weight than used to mend tears—that is the length and width of the spine area. This will stabilize the backs of the sections and begin to hold the spine rigid.

While the spine linings dry, I make new endbands for the book. In the early days of bookbinding, the endbands consisted of a core of leather or cord that was sewn onto the top and bottom of the text block with a series of windings of thread to wrap it. They were tacked periodically through the section folds below, and helped protect the head and tail of the text block's spine. Fine bindings still use ornate endbands made this way using colored silks. Usually for conservation work, I sew new endbands of unbleached linen thread. But in the early nineteenth century, when *Campaign* was published, endbands consisted of pieces of striped cloth folded over a cord core, cut to the width of the text block, and glued onto the book at the head and tail. Like two-on sewing, this type of "stuck-on" endband significantly speeded up the binding process. Since I am putting a new cover on this book, I choose to put on a new endband that approximates what *Campaign* might have had originally.

I take a small piece of unbleached linen and dilute a little forest green acrylic paint in a glass bowl. Using the edge of a plastic drafting triangle, I paint thin, evenly spaced stripes on the linen. I have made endbands like this before and it goes quickly. When the piece of linen is dry, I glue it in half with a piece of cord inside the fold. When the new endband material is dry, I cut off two widths and glue them on the text block—still in the press—at the head and tail with PVA, a heavier adhesive. Then I line the spine with PVA and three more layers of handmade cotton paper running the length of the spine and the endbands. There are three slight bulges in the paper linings where they run over the sewing tapes. When the linings are dry, I sand these areas lightly until the entire spine is flush and smooth. Forwarding complete, the book is now ready for covering, and I take it out of the job backer.

○ ○ ○

Periodically, Bill brought items of special interest down from Special Collections for us to look at during class. It was a chance to examine styles of bindings that we would never get the chance to make in class. One night he showed us a jeweled binding (a copy of *King Florus and the Fair Jehane*). I knew such bindings existed, but had never seen one up close. It was covered in green leather with a fine gold filigree decorating the edges of the boards, set with tiny opals and rubies. But the ornate binding also kept the book from opening easily. This was obviously a case in which the binding mattered more than the content of the book inside.

Another night, I remember that we were all hard at work when Bill asked quietly if we would like to see a page from the Gutenberg Bible. Suddenly everyone was standing around the middle workbench as he opened a tall black leather-covered book—a slender volume containing an essay about the Gutenberg Bible in general and this single page in particular. I had never seen a leaf-book before and was amazed that we were looking at a page from the famous forty-two-line Bible, the first book printed in Europe.

It was a beautiful, creamy page with dark type in two heavy columns. Bill let us examine both sides and touch it. I had no idea that our own Special Collections held such an item.

"Why would just one page be bound up like this?" someone asked.

"It's a presentation binding," Bill answered. "Incomplete copies of famous and valuable books are cut up and sold as single sheets. Dealers can get more money for the pages individually than they can for the volume as an incomplete copy of something."

I was appalled. It seem barbaric to cut up a text—even if it wasn't complete.

Another time Bill showed us a magnificent illuminated book of hours that he was going to rebind—a fifteenth-century French manuscript that had been horribly mutilated. None of us had seen a book like this before. Bill paged through it carefully, his hands supporting the fragmented pages, to show us the one remaining illustration and the pages where the other illuminated capitals and decorative borders had been cut out. Slowly he turned pages that resembled Swiss cheese. So much material had been cut away that in places only stubs of text remained along the gutter. Apparently such treatment had once been common practice. Victorians kept "border books" of the illustrations and decorative borders they had cut from manuscripts. I was amazed that people would brutalize such obvious works of art. I could see that part of conservation was coming to terms with such injuries. But how do you compensate in a text for things that were missing or removed? Bill told us he planned to inlay new, blank pieces of vellum, restoring the integrity of the manuscript pages so that readers could more easily turn them to enjoy the beauty that remained.

○ ○ ○

I line two pieces of binder's cardboard with acid-free paper on each side to add stability, cutting them down to the size I want for the covers. I have to allow enough extra for the "square" of the boards—that strip that sticks out beyond the edges of the text block. A spacer strip of cord is glued down on what will become the inner edge of each board. This will be removed after the leather cover of the book has dried and will keep the hinge area from becoming too tight as the leather shrinks and dries on the book.

I fit the boards on the book and use PVA to glue the tapes to the inside of the boards. When they dry, I paste three layers of a thin, hard machine-made paper over them, ending the paper just past the edges of the tapes. When this too is dry, I sand the paper smooth so that there are no ridges from the tapes. I press the book—with the boards now attached—under weight for several days to help the book and board adjust to their new configuration.

While *Campaign* is under weight, I prepare the leather for covering it. I cut a piece of dark brown calf from a large skin and shave the edges thin with a French bookbinder's paring knife. When I had first learned to pare leather, my specimens resembled lasagna noodles—flat in the middle with waves along the edges from being stretched by the blade. Now I can pare well enough to take the thickness off the edge neatly. Keeping my knife extremely sharp helps.

In the areas where the leather needs to be slightly thinner—such as in the hinge areas or at the corners where the leather will fold back on top of itself—I use a spokeshave to pare the leather. Bookbinding and conservation make a practice of borrowing and adapting tools from other professions. This is a regular woodworker's spokeshave—a plane with handles on both sides—from Sears. I have reground and sharpened the blade, shaping it for leatherwork. Paring leather is a tricky process, and I have to proceed carefully or I will nick holes in the leather. I once went through five strips of leather while preparing a leather spine piece for a binding. This paring, however, goes quickly.

I stir up a bowl of cold-water paste that doesn't have to be cooked, mixing it with water until I get the consistency of oatmeal. I don't need a paste as pure (or as expensive) as *ɀin shofu* for this step. The paste will be trapped away from the text block. I also lay out the brushes, knives, and other materials I will need to put the leather on the book.

Lifting the book from under the weights, I wrap the text block with waste paper to protect it from the paste. With a wad of cotton, I dampen the leather from the right side with some water. This will put moisture into the skin and keep the first application of paste from drying out completely. With a large brush, I then paste out the leather. I fold the piece gently in half without creasing it and let it sit for a minute or two. Then I scrape off all the paste and apply a second layer. The previous application has charged the skin with water, allowing the new layer of paste to stay tacky and workable. I lay the book down onto the leather and begin to work the skin onto the book. I wish I had two more hands.

This step requires dexterity and patience. The leather must be turned over the edges and slipped down in a neat tuck behind the endbands. The corner areas must be pared again while wet and folded over into neat pleats that will protect the corners of the covers. All of this must be done carefully—wet leather marks easily—and it must be done before the leather and paste dry out. I always find it a nerve-racking procedure, rather like getting all the dishes for Thanksgiving prepared and on the table at the same time.

Once I have finished, a piece of card—a "fence"—is slipped inside each cover, extending beyond its edges to keep moisture from migrating from the wet leather into the text block. I wrap the book with a piece of felt to keep it from getting marked and weight it under a board to dry overnight.

○ ○ ○

As I continued to take Bill's class each semester, I tried to figure out where I could go to continue my bookbinding studies. Even though I had advanced to become Kim's printing assistant at Windhover, my experiences with Bill convinced me that my passion lay in binding rather than printing. I preferred restoring books one at a time to printing them in batches of two hundred and fifty. I asked Kim one day if he knew where

I could go to study. Somewhere in Europe perhaps? I was certain I could convince my husband to continue his own graduate studies abroad for a year.

"You could go to Camberwell in England," he replied, "but why would you want to leave Iowa City when one of the best bookbinders and conservators in the business is across the parking lot in the library?"

I explained to him how taking a class that only met once a week was great, but that there was so much more I wanted to learn. It would take forever at such a snail's pace.

"Well, maybe Bill will ask you to be his next apprentice," Kim replied. "But your work will have to be exceptional, and you'll have to impress him with your attitude. He's never taken a woman as an apprentice before."

Yes, that was one thing that had been made clear to me by this time. Bill had always had only male apprentices. The tradition under which he had trained in Ireland was male dominated. Women only worked in the shops sewing books. Men trained as apprentices with a master and moved on in the profession, often serving as journeymen, until they were masters themselves. This was the course Bill had followed.

"Mark's apprenticeship with Bill will be up this fall," Kim continued. "He'll have to think of taking on someone new." Mark Esser was apprenticed to Bill when he had moved to Iowa City from Chicago. One of Bill's agreements with the university was that Mark would move too, receive a salary, and be able to finish his training. Now in the spring of 1986,

Mark was beginning to look for a job. "You'll just have to show Bill you're interested," Kim finished.

I was indeed interested and thought for days about the possibility of becoming an apprentice. But how would I go about convincing Bill that I could be a good one? And would he even consider me? Early in the semester, one Wednesday night after class over a beer at a local microbrewery, he had told me of a woman who had asked to be his apprentice whom he had turned down. At the time he told me the story, I wasn't sure that he had refused her because she wasn't talented enough or because she was a woman. This was not encouraging.

Even now I am not sure *what* I did to convince Bill that I would be a good choice for an apprentice. The previous semester he had asked me in passing if I was interested in studying bookbinding—he knew from conversations that we had had about my work at Windhover that printing was not going to be my life's profession—but I was also working on a Ph.D. in English literature and was teaching rhetoric. I was in Iowa so that I could teach writing someday.

I only know that I worked very hard in class and was meticulous in my work. I made plans to continue learning as much as possible about book arts and signed up to take a class in the fall with Tim Barrett, the papermaker Kim had just brought to the university. I figured that if I were going to spend all this time making books out of paper, it would be to my advantage to know more about its properties and how it was made. Before I began working at Windhover, paper was just paper. Then it gradually became a vehicle for impressing type, distinct in color and surface texture. Now I knew that there were papers made and used just for conservation techniques. Tim Barrett was one of the foremost producers of those papers.

◦ ◦ ◦

The next day I take *Campaign* out from under the weight and remove it from the felt. The leather looks smooth and dry across the cover. With a wet swab, I dampen the hinge area from the outside and open both the front and back covers, acquainting the leather with this movement. I remove the fences and strip the spacer cord with tweezers. Finally, I remove the waste-paper wrap from around the text block.

Now it is time to finish the covering. I take a scalpel and ruler and carefully trim the leather turn-ins on the inside of the covers so that they form a neat rectangle. The leather forms a slight ridge that would be noticeable under a pastedown, so I cut a thin piece of card to the exact size and glue it into the opening. Then I glue out the linen hinge that is wrapped around the end section of new paper that I had added to the text and work it across the hinge area and onto the inside of the cover, smoothing it flat with my bone folder. The book is dried open for a few minutes, then shut. I cut a piece of paper for the pastedown that matches the new endpapers and glue it down to the inside of the board, again slipping in the piece of card back to act as a moisture barrier, and weight the book for a few minutes more to allow the pastedown to adhere. I repeat the procedure for the other cover and place the book back under weight.

While the pastedowns dry, I set up the tooling stove on my bench. This affair is similar to an electric hotplate with a fixed ring like a halo that surrounds it and supports the finishing tools. These roughly resemble screwdrivers. Usually they are made up of rounded wood handles with a brass extension. The brass is shaped on the tip into numerous ornate flowers, lines, curves, and alphabets. I lay out a piece of line that will be used to make the decorative rules across the spine of the book, dividing it into the traditional five panels.

The endpapers dry just as the stove is hot. I place the book in the finishing press—a wooden press that holds the book clamped spine up for tooling—with felt wrapped around it to protect it from pressure marks. The spine is parallel to the edge of my bench. I test the heat of the tool by touching the brass to a wet sponge in a bowl, and it hisses briefly. I have marked out the spine of the book with evenly spaced needle pricks to show me where to make the lines. Single lines at top and bottom, double lines to divide the panels in the traditional style. I wrap a piece of thin card over the curve of the spine as a guide and place the edge of the tool against it. Quickly, I roll the polished surface of the line across the back of the spine in one smooth motion. I step back to see how it turned out. A nice even line blind embossed into the leather. I reheat the tool briefly, cool it down on the sponge, and tool the rest of the panel divisions. They go well and most are complete on the first pass.

Once I have tooled the lines, I dampen them one at a time with a small piece of cotton, retooling them with the heated piece of line. The moisture and leather react together to leave a blackened mark in the leather. This adds more definition to the impression.

Tooling leather like this is a another nerve-racking business. It is very easy to have the tool too hot or to emboss too deeply. It is also very easy to have the tool so hot it burns completely through the leather to the spine lining paper below. I did this once. Fortunately, it was in the second panel from the top where the lettering of the title of the book traditionally goes. I simply put a piece of colored leather in that panel and tooled the title into that. Such overlabeling is a common practice among binders and it looked nice when I was finished. I wonder how many books with labels onlaid onto leather spines had other crispy lettering underneath? Dampening and darkening these spine lines goes quickly.

When I have finished my tooling, I prepare the original label from the spine of *Campaign* that I had saved. It is a fairly thick but weakened leather. With my lifting knives I gently scrape away excess material from the back, thinning it down. Because of the condition of the leather this is done easily, although I must be careful not to chip off pieces at the edges. I paste a layer of the Japanese mending tissue to the back to strengthen it. When this is dry, I glue the label into the second panel from the top of the new binding. Since I had calculated the size of the panels according to the length of this label, it's a perfect fit.

The conservation of this book is now complete, and I will make it a protective box before it goes back to Special Collections. This work has taken several weeks to complete. I lean over my workbench, pull out the book's treatment survey sheet, and begin to complete the sections on what has been done to *Campaign*.

○ ○ ○

I will never forget that early March evening. I was working at one of the end benches putting the cover on a book for my father, when Bill suddenly faced me from the other side of the bench. Usually when he wanted to see what I was doing he came up next to me. He wasn't smiling, but looked very intent standing there in his usual khaki pants and pinstriped oxford shirt, sleeves rolled up just below the elbows.

"How would you like to become my next apprentice?"

Suddenly a large pit opened up in the bottom of my stomach. How did he know what I wanted more than anything? He was really asking *me*—a woman—to become his apprentice. I couldn't believe it. I took a deep breath and answered him.

I told him no.

Not no, I didn't want to be his apprentice. But no, I couldn't do it right away. I explained that I still had a year left of my agreement with Kim to be his printing assistant for two years. I explained to Bill that I didn't want to go back on my word even though his offer was tempting. I told him that I had signed up to take papermaking because I thought a knowledge of how paper was made would make me a better bookbinder. On and on I babbled, blowing my chances, letting myself and all of womanhood down. The pit in my stomach, born of excitement, was now hard and cold.

When I had finished, Bill stood there for a moment and said, "All right. I can understand your obligation to Kim. How would you like to start as soon as the next school year is over?"

Calmly, I told him that would be fine. He said that he would just find someone else who could start first. He turned and walked away. I went quietly back to work, putting the cover on my father's book upside down.

TOOLS

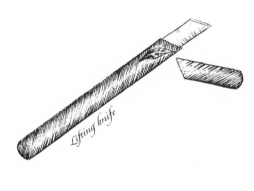

Lifting knife

Bookbinders are a scavenger breed. They pore through art, jewelry, and woodworking supply catalogues, looking for tools they might adopt and adapt to bookbinding. Bookbinding catalogues are filled with tools borrowed from other professions and crafts. Jewelers' clamps and saws, doctors' hemostats and scalpels, woodworkers' spokeshaves and block planes—often altered by the purchaser in ways that marry them forever after to bookbinding.

One morning, early in my apprenticeship, Bill came down to my workbench at the other end of the Conservation Department and laid down a fine-toothed hacksaw blade. I could not remember ever seeing Bill use a hacksaw while binding a book, and I looked up at him. He smiled at my confusion. "It's so you can make your own set of lifting knives," he said. "Let me know when you're ready to begin."

I had been in Bill's night class for more than two years before beginning my apprenticeship, and I was becoming more perceptive about his techniques of instruction. I knew that by giving me the blade in this manner, he wanted me to think about what to do next with this thin, flexible piece of metal. I went over to Bill's bench and took out his set of lifting

47

knives—used to lift leather on the spines and covers of books during conservation treatments—and returned to my bench to study them.

Bill kept his tools in two sets of cast-off library card catalogue drawers that sat on the back right-hand corner of his bench. Each drawer displayed a rectangular brass holder bearing a slip of paper that in one or two words categorized the tools inside: "knives," "folders," "sewing." It was understood that his apprentices were allowed access to these tools. It was also understood that we were to use them carefully and return them to their proper drawer as soon as we were finished. Once we acquired a particular hand tool of our own, we stopped using Bill's.

Often the handles of Bill's tools—such as the knives and scalpels—had been wrapped with dark strips of pared book leather to make them more comfortable to hold. The leather was darkened by years of being used and held, years of oil from his hands. They had a certain feel to them. A smooth professionalism.

In the early stages of using my own newly apprenticed tools, I would go to the drawers and get Bill's paper knife or bone folder—especially if I was having difficulties with my own. His tools were smarter than mine. They knew the correct way to cut paper or pare leather. By using them I could feel in my hands how the tools were supposed to work. Then I would go back to my own paper knife or bone folder, feel the imperfections in the way it worked, and try to correct them. Someday I wanted my tools to be as smart as Bill's.

As I began to prepare my lifting knives from the hacksaw blade, Bill gave me a video and a book to study that contained information on sharpening blades. This was uncharacteristic of him. He had learned bookbinding from his father in Ireland in a traditional apprenticeship, later serving as a journeyman binder. He believed you learned this craft from watching and emulating, not from reading the scores of available books, so I was surprised that he had given me these materials. In retrospect, it was probably because his knives (all with years of service) would not need the type of shaping and sharpening I was about to undertake.

The video he gave me was of a session filmed at one of the annual Guild of Book Workers Standards Seminars—David Brock demonstrating knife sharpening. I took it to the library's Microtext Reading Room and spent a long morning watching the badly recorded tape, trying to decipher what David was saying and showing. I was also intrigued because David had been an apprentice of Bill's in Chicago before Bill moved to Iowa to develop the university's Conservation Department. I had heard stories and anecdotes about David and privately considered him a relative (an older brother who had already left home). I could see a great similarity between David's meticulous attention to detail and Bill's.

The video gave me a good idea of what I needed to do to sharpen my lifting knives using a series of Japanese water stones. These stones are much like the oil stones commonly used for sharpening. My father had had an oil stone on his workbench in the garage, and he periodically doused the stone with 3-In-1 Oil before sharpening the hedge clippers.

But these Japanese water stones are smooth rectangles, red stone of different grits that use water, not oil, for a lubricant. A far cry from my father's coarse, irregular gray slab. And obviously I wanted a better edge on my lifting knives than my father had wanted on his hedge clippers. So I turned to the next source Bill had given me: *Japanese Woodworking Tools: Their Tradition, Spirit and Use,* by Toshio Ōdate.

In this book, Ōdate instructs Western woodworkers in the care and use of Japanese woodworking tools, based on his own apprenticeship as a teenager to become a *tategu-shi,* a sliding-door maker. His training was spiritual as well as technical, and his cultural reverence for handcraft and the tradition in which he learned it permeates the instructions in the text.

Ōdate was apprenticed to his stepfather—quite unusual in Japanese tradition. Fathers usually apprentice their sons to other craftsmen—except in cases such as swordsmiths, whose methods of forging blades are secret and thus are passed down only from father to son. On the first day of his apprenticeship, Ōdate's stepfather disowned him so that he would not have to treat his stepson with paternal respect. This allowed Ōdate's stepfather to rebuke him verbally and physically in the customary manner of such apprenticeships.

In reading the first chapters of this book, long before I got to the sixth chapter on sharpening, I was hooked. I had delayed for a year the beginning of my apprenticeship with Bill to study papermaking. During those studies, I had been intrigued with *nagashi-zuki,* the traditional methods of Japanese papermaking. I had spent more time studying and producing Japanese kozo papers than I had spent with Western papermaking. I had worked diligently while forming sheets to try and develop *kan*—the ability to judge intuitively. To know just by running my hand through the vat when the slurry (the mixture of water and kozo fiber) had reached the right consistency. To know when my techniques were right just by the way the water danced across the papermold as the sheet was formed. Now Ōdate was telling me about the Japanese apprenticeship system, building on the groundwork of my appreciation for the Japanese approach to craftsmanship.

I was captured by his thoughts on apprenticeship. I knew my experience would be vastly different from the medieval bookbinding apprenticeships, in which the apprentice—always male—lived with his master's family, receiving room, board, and clothing. Different, too, from the apprenticeship Bill had served in Ireland with his father. Different from the apprentices—all male—that Bill had trained before me in his Chicago shop and in Iowa. And different from Ōdate's experience in a country and craft far removed from my own. But I was curious about apprenticeship and what it implied about the relationship Bill and I would develop over the next five to seven years. And I felt a strong affinity with Ōdate's respect for his tools and his reverence toward the apprenticeship system.

Ōdate, in the course of his apprenticeship, became a *shokunin*—a word that translates as "craftsman" or "artisan." But he explains that the term embraces much more. A *shokunin* demonstrates great knowledge of the tools he uses, creating beauty through his work. But there is also a philosophical component to such mastery of a craft. Ōdate observes that a *shokunin* imbues his work with his soul, taking great pride in his craftsmanship. As I watched Bill work every day, this rang true for me. He performed each step of a conservation treatment carefully, with consideration as to how the finished item would continue to be housed and used. I never saw him rush through a task or complete one sloppily.

I continued to read and think about Ōdate's book, finding strong philosophical parallels as I compared my apprenticeship to his, though we each were instructed in different manners. Bill and I never discussed the book beyond the details of using the Japanese water stones. But I began to see him as a *shokunin*—and to hear Ōdate in my mind.

○ ○ ○

For the *shokunin*, utility and appearance must be enhanced by a tool's "presence," that is its refinement and dignity. . . . Presence is what the toolmaker . . . imbues his creation with as a result of his commitment to his craft; it is the spirit of the tool that records the *shokunin*'s ability through the years to face the uncertainties of life, to overcome them, and to master the art of living. (179)

Lifting knives are used for a variety of tasks—lifting old leather from the spines of volumes that need to be rebacked, slicing paper linings from their spines—anything where a thin, flexible blade has an advantage. A hacksaw blade is the perfect raw material for their construction.

I had borrowed Bill's lifting knives many times and was thrilled to be making a set for myself. It seemed to me that if I made my own knives, I would know them better than a knife I had bought. They would work better.

I remembered ordering my French paring knife—a beautiful blade of polished steel set into a wooden handle. I had spent hours sharpening it, wrapping the handle in leather, and making a protective cover so that the blade wouldn't get nicked in my drawer. But as sharp and beautiful as it was, sometimes it seemed to have a mind of its own, slicing completely through leather I just wanted to pare. It had a volatile temperament.

The first step in transforming a hacksaw blade into lifting knives was to snap the blade in half. Bill had me mark the halfway point on the blade at a forty-five-degree angle. This was easily done. But at that point, I stood at my bench wondering how to break the flexible metal in half. I went to Bill with my question.

"Ah, that's easy," he smiled. He took me back down the length of the department to the large job backer near my bench. This is a large, standing book press that grips books, spine up, so that they can be worked on.

Bill took my hacksaw and clamped it in the job backer, the forty-five-degree line even with the jaws of the press. He spun the wheel that tightened them, clamping the blade tight. "There," he said. "Now we'll just snap it in half."

Bill lifted a heavy pair of pliers off the pegboard, grabbed the blade close to where it was clamped, and with a quick downward motion, snapped the metal in half. He made it look easy.

"Now what you need to do is file the teeth off the edges of the knives." He proceeded back to the counter and from a cabinet underneath pulled out an electric grinding stone. He plugged it in and filled the reservoir with tap water. "You'll need to plunge your knives into the water periodically to cool them down," he said. "The friction of the stone can make them too hot." He gave me the pliers so that I could hold each blade with two hands, demonstrated briefly, and then left me to the roar of the grinding wheel.

○ ○ ○

This then, is the equipment in the *shokunin*'s workshop. You may begin to see that the *shokunin*'s art is difficult, if not impossible, to separate from his work space, his tools and his equipment. The craft is not apart from his life so much as it is a heightened detail of life. (11)

As I watched Bill work on a daily basis, rather than just one night a week in class, I appreciated his manner of working and teaching. He did everything as well as it could possibly be done, but without spending more time on a task than was necessary.

The tools and equipment that we used in the department had been Bill's when he had his bindery in Chicago. I had always assumed that the library had purchased them when he came to the university. Only after his death did I learn that this was not the case. He had made an agreement that the university would one day purchase his tools, but the transaction had never actually taken place. Then I appreciated even more his cavalier attitude about letting us use all of the equipment roughly in the manner of beginners.

From the first time I had set foot in the department, I had been fascinated by its equipment. The large board shears and guillotine for cutting paper and boards. The futuristic ultra-sonic welder (invented by a previous apprentice of Bill's) for encapsulating fragile book pages and documents between sheets of clear Mylar. The large standing presses, the finishing presses, and the job backers. Each with its own function and vocabulary: "nipping between boards," "tying up," "rounding and backing." Sometimes I would tease Bill by deliberately mangling terminology because he liked us to be precise. When nipping a book in the press to adhere it to its new cover, I would ask Bill in consultation if I should "munch it awhile in the press." He would make a face and tell me yes, "give it a good munch." Later I would show it to him, commenting on how well it had all "smashed together."

I had a healthy respect and fear of the board shears and

guillotine. When I had worked for a small hand-bindery in town, I managed at one point to cut my hands twice in as many weeks on the large cutters in the shop. One day while I was alone trimming board for covers, I simply lifted the back of my hand up into the long, sharp blade of the board shear, not even feeling it slice cleanly through my skin. I couldn't find any Band-Aids and ended up getting someone to drive me to the emergency room, my hand wrapped tightly in a tea towel. A week or so later, again while cutting board, I nicked the back of my other hand in a ragged tear on the sharp corner of the guillotine blade. The cut was deep, but not nearly as bloody as the previous incision. I never cut myself on a large blade again, having learned the hard way to always keep an eye on the relationship of the blade to my hands.

Bill was much more protective of his personal hand tools than he was with the big equipment. He was upset at one point when through overuse his apprentices and students had worn down the various tiny punches of his Japanese screw-punch, a tool that we used to drill small holes through leather, vellum, and paper. A friend in Japan had sent it as a gift after Bill had seen him use it and had expressed admiration for its simplicity and usefulness. Larry Yerkes, Bill's other apprentice, who had begun his training the year before I had, eventually arranged for us to order more of these tools from a distributor in Japan (a long process involving a translator and many trips to the bank to figure out exchange rates) so that we could replace Bill's punches and each have a set of our own.

After Bill died, the university purchased the large equipment and a number of smaller tools from his wife, Bernie. His daughters came and emptied his tool drawers of those that they wanted. They took the beloved, leather-wrapped tools he had used for so many years, leaving behind other, perhaps less cherished items. Slowly, over the course of many weeks, Larry and I and Sally—one of Bill's last-chosen apprentices—claimed our tools of remembrance. I selected a French paring knife and a small, thin metal spatula, their handles wrapped but not darkened from use. A small saw with several interchangeable blades. An extra spokeshave blade. A Japanese plane block that Bill had seasoned with oil but only used once. A set of Japanese gimlets for drilling tiny holes. And a wonderful, wooden-handled device that I had often used to remove rusty staples from pamphlets. In fact, I used it so often that Bill finally had told me to keep it in my drawers. It had a round, almost ballish wooden handle and a short, dull blade that slipped easily under staples without marring the paper underneath. It had been given to him by Elizabeth Kner, the Hungarian binder who had been his partner in Chicago before her retirement. I had never considered that it was another adopted tool until one day someone asked if they could borrow my "oyster knife" to remove some staples.

❖ ❖ ❖

> When I was an apprentice, we made [*shirabiki*] . . . knives our-
> selves from old hacksaw blades or small, worn-out flat files,
> because after the war it was difficult to purchase them. (29)

Once I had ground the teeth off the blade halves, I asked Bill
what the next step would be. "We'll quickly take the angle of
the knife back on the grinding stone," he said, "and then you
can do the rest of the finishing by hand." He headed once
again for the back counter.

This time he held the blade in his hand, turned on the
grinding stone, and at the forty-five-degree edge of the knife,
ground it back to shape its sloped cutting edge. It took only
seconds. He turned to me, "You do the next one and then put
the grinding stone away."

It took me several attempts and many minutes to grind
the blade of the other lifting knife, leaving one knife half an
inch shorter than the other. It was the same experience I always
have with an electric pencil sharpener: by the time I get a
good point, most of the pencil is gone. I was glad to put the
grinder away. Electric tools do things too quickly, leaving me
no time to spot errors and finesse my way out of them.

When I was still taking Bill's class, I had purchased a yellow plastic Fiskars hand drill to drill sewing holes in wooden
boards. I had tried using the electric one in the department and
had ruined a wooden cover by drilling holes too quickly in the
wrong places. With the hand drill, I never made such mistakes.

I went back to my bench and again examined Bill's knives. I realized that before I made handles and covers for them, I needed to sharpen the cutting edge and polish the sides. I got out the Japanese sharpening stones and set them to soak in a bucket of water, tiny air bubbles rising quickly to the surface.

Originally, Japanese swordsmiths used stones quarried from special areas to sharpen their blades, each stone named for the stratum it came from. Even today, Japan still has famous quarries known for the sharpening stones they produce for woodworkers and other professionals. But these stones are prohibitively expensive, so most craftsmen now use man-made stones. They come in uniform shapes and sizes and are easy to buy and construct holders for.

When Bill purchased three water stones of varying grits for the department, he assigned me the task of making a holder for them. We laminated a piece of wood to make it waterproof. Then, using brass screws, I attached two pieces of oak finished with boat-deck sealer to make the front and back stops for the stones. The stones slipped into this, and the whole board fit into the top of the sink. That way the water poured over the stones and went down the drain.

Once the stones were saturated, I placed the coarsest grit stone in the holder. Since I had already ground the edge on the knives, it was just a matter of polishing them to smooth out imperfections. As I moved each blade back and forth in a long, even stroke across the top of the oblong, red water stone, I periodically poured a little more water on the surface to act as a lubricant for the blade. If not kept wet, the pores of the stone will clog with tiny particles of metal. Keeping the surface clean allows the stone to cut faster. I could tell that the blade edge was honed when the minute scratch lines across its surface from the stone were clean and unbroken by any dips in its surface. Then I rinsed off the stone and replaced it with the stone of the next-finest grit.

By the time I finished with the third and finest stone, the cutting edges of the lifting knives had smooth, polished surfaces. I repeated the procedure on the top two inches of the front and back sides of both blades as well. The sides of a knife need to be polished smooth so that they offer no resistance when moved over the material to be cut. My blades now matched the clean, finished look of Bill's. Next I was ready to make their handles.

○ ○ ○

> The toolbox . . . is also a resting place for the *shokunin*'s tools and thus a symbol of the *shokunin*. It is sometimes said that a *shokunin*'s ability need not be measured by an examination of his work—a look inside his toolbox is enough. (10)

Each apprentice worked to develop a personal set of tools. I had been building mine gradually since I first enrolled in Bill's classes. I began with a single bone folder—a long, slender, flat piece of polished bone used primarily to sharpen creases when folding paper—that had been given to me by Kay

Amert when I took her typography class at the university in the summer of 1981.

Kay's class gave me the opportunity to create my first book from beginning to end, composing the text, designing the page layout, setting the type, printing the folios, and binding the books. In my senior year at the University of California at San Diego, I had taken a class in profile writing. For my term project, I had gone underground to investigate and interview UCSD's group of graffiti artists—the Wall Writers—who haunted the cold and sterile concrete staircases of some of the university's newer buildings. Unlike sporadic graffiti artists, the Wall Writers had personae and pen names, and held continuing conversations with each other. For my final typography project for Kay's class, I had chosen to set some of this graffiti in various typefaces that reflected in size and style their content.

In one of the last demonstrations during that course, Kay had shown us how to do a simple full-cloth case binding. This was my first binding lesson. As her hands moved through the steps of the simple case construction, I was attracted to the tool she kept using to construct the cover (a bone folder). After she was finished, I picked it up. It was cool, but warmed immediately in my hands.

"Where can I get one of these?" I asked her.

"You can't buy them here in town," she replied. "Just keep this one," she said.

It was the generous act of a good teacher. It was my first

bookbinding tool and one of my most cherished. In fact, bone folders became my favorite tool.

They are one of the tools most often used by bookbinders and book and paper conservators. Made of bone from the leg of a cow, they resemble a rounded tongue depressor. They come rounded on both ends, or with one point shaped to a gradual point. They are essential for sharpening the crease in folds of paper. They can also be used to score thin card, rub down papers being adhered, work leather onto a book, and shape the rounding of a spine. Often the bone folders we bought from binding suppliers were too thick to do the fine work required of them.

Bill had a lovely bone folder that I often borrowed for leatherwork. It was thinner than a normal folder with a tapering point. It also had a translucent quality to it. "Why don't you make your own folder like this?" he asked me one morning, when I was borrowing his.

"How do I do that?"

"Do you have any spare folders?" he asked. When I nodded, he said, "Let's take a look."

At my bench, I took out the two spare folders I had in my tackle box and handed them to Bill. He immediately chose the smaller of the two and said, "This will work perfectly. First, you'll have to grind it down a bit." Out came the grinding wheel from under the back counter.

"You want to grind down one side of this to narrow it down. You want a width that will feel nice in your hand, with a point that's narrow enough to be controlled by one finger. When you finish that, flatten the broad surface of the point by hand on some sandpaper. Then let me see it."

I filled the water reservoir and turned on the grinder. I began to move the width of the bone across the wheel. Quickly a sickening smell began to fill the room. Even though I dunked it in the water reservoir repeatedly, the bone got hot as it was ground away. The room began to smell like burned hair. My stomach began to get queasy. I noticed Larry opening the windows along the wall of benches.

"What is that *awful* smell?" one of the librarians asked from the other side of the cage. I hurried to finish grinding. "It's like the smell when the dentist drills your teeth too long," someone else said.

When I had finished all my sanding, I took the folder back to Bill. "This looks about right," he said. "You have a nice thin point now that will work well for leather." I had taken the point thickness down from an eighth of an inch to a sixteenth.

"How do I get it translucent like yours?" I asked.

"Well, traditionally," he explained, "you would use your folder so much that the oils from your hand would turn it translucent gradually. But there's a quicker way to do it." Bill went to the filing cabinet where we kept the tooling supplies and brought out a small bottle of oil. "Rub a little of this on it, wrap it in some plastic, and leave it overnight."

The next morning when I unwrapped it, I had a thin and delicate new bone folder. "That looks nice," Bill said, upon examining it. "The oil will keep adhesives from sticking to it and help it glide over the leather."

By the time I finished my apprenticeship, I owned twelve folders of various sizes, shapes, and functions, some that I had adapted myself, each with a different function. I had bone folders, brass folders (used for scoring card and thin board), and even a Teflon folder. Teflon was a popular new material for folders because it could be cut to shape easily and sanded quickly by hand. It glided over any surface without leaving a mark. I liked my Teflon folder, but found that because it was softer than bone, it wasn't stiff enough for numerous tasks that I preferred bone for. You also had to wear a mask while sanding it because it was dangerous to inhale the Teflon particles. I knew one conservator who had been taken quite ill as a result of making a Teflon folder. I preferred bone folders.

As I acquired more and more tools, I needed something to store them in. At the beginning of Larry's apprenticeship, he had gotten a set of surplus card catalogue drawers like Bill's for his bench. Sally had inherited a similar set from a previous work-study student. Lisa, Bill's youngest daughter and also a work-study student in the department, had been given the last set. It was in such bad condition that she had covered it with a purple-and-blue marbled paper to hide all the stains and scratches.

When I started in the department, there were no extra drawer sets available in the library storage area. For several months I stored my tools in the small, blue tackle box that I had used to carry my tools back and forth to class one night a week.

But one Saturday at an antique show, I discovered a set of large, cherry drawers. I fell in love with their warm red color and bought them on the spot. They even separated into two-drawered tiers to make them easier to carry. I set them up in the department the very next day, dispersing my tools into the drawers. Although they had bulged out of the tackle box, they seemed very small in the cherry drawers. On Monday morning I was sliding labels into the brass holders when Bill and Larry arrived. At last, my bench looked like everyone else's.

That fall and spring, I continued to fill my drawers with tools that I made or bought and adapted. When I began my apprenticeship, my blue tackle box held a bone folder, a boxing knife for cutting paper, scissors, needles, a straightedge, a scalpel, and some sewing thread wound around a piece of card. When I finished my training five years later, I took my tools home in my cherry drawers and two packing boxes. (This did not include the portfolios of my paper stock that had been in one of the department's flat files, or the boxes of my notes, files, and other binding odds and ends.) I had spent so much time sharpening my knives that I developed carpal tunnel syndrome in both wrists and had to have them operated on, one a summer, for two years. I took toolmaking to heart.

So much to heart, in fact, that my husband began to cringe every time he saw the latest Daniel Smith art supply catalogue or Garrett Wade woodworking tool catalogue arrive in the mail. He knew that I would shortly begin my campaign for budgeting "just one tool this month." A palm plane for rounding corners of wooden covers. A lining brush to use with water to wet-tear small strips of mending paper. A snail-shaped sanding block, complete with rolls of sticky-backed adhesive of varying grits (much more versatile than a regular rectangular sanding block, I explained to him). After awhile he began to tease me that I had become a binder just because I liked to buy tools.

Sally and I combed through the catalogues, trading wish lists back and forth. Someone in the department would order a new tool, and soon everyone else would try it and buy one. Often we would circulate catalogues and send in large group orders to save on postage and handling.

Besides the hand tools in our drawers, there were many more tools we shared in the department that were stored on pegboards, in drawers, stacked in glass-fronted cabinets. That was one aspect of working in Conservation that took me a long time to learn—where everything was kept. Bill had even had a special rack built over the back counter to house the long-handled rolls and hand tools used for tooling leather. Visitors to the department asked us if we used them, since often people collect and hang them on the wall for decoration.

It soon became apparent to me that some people in the shop treated our common tools with more respect and care than others did. This was especially true for the brushes.

Behind the sink on the counter in the back of the room were several tall plastic cups that held the collection of brushes we used daily. There were large oval elephant brushes that held lots of adhesive for gluing out and casing in books, or for gluing out large pieces of book cloth. Smaller domed brushes were used for other gluing jobs such as pasting out book spines. We had assorted small brushes that were used to color cloth and dye leather. And there were the Japanese *hake* brushes with very soft bristles used to apply paste when backing fragile paper with thin sheets of kozo. After we used the brushes, we were expected to clean them by rubbing the wet bristles across a piece of Ivory soap, housed in an old china cup. Then we were to rinse the brushes and stand them upside down in one of the plastic cups to dry.

A good idea, but some people were better than others about washing out their brushes. Occasionally I would prepare to glue something out only to discover that the brush I had chosen had last been used for coloring and hadn't been washed very well. Sally got angry when she grabbed one of the large elephant brushes that hadn't been cleaned thoroughly, resulting in bristles glued stiff. She would stand in the back of the room and pound the bristles on the counter so that we could hear the hard sound they made. This situation got worse as library interns and new student workers came and went in the department.

Eventually, Sally and I bought our own sets of brushes that we kept on our benches. I bought a cake of artist's brush soap that helped condition their bristles. I stopped using the common brushes altogether. By unspoken agreement, Sally and I shared brushes and other tools. We treated each other's tools with the same respect we treated our own.

○ ○ ○

The bond between the *shokunin* and his tools is not only practical but emotional and spiritual; this bond, once experienced, is not easily ignored or changed. (10)

It is difficult to work holding a bare metal blade, so it was necessary for me to put handles on my lifting knives. Most blades are set into some sort of wooden handles, but because lifting knives are often used almost parallel to the surface you're working on, I needed something with a lower profile and more flexible than wood.

Bill's lifting knives were covered with leather over card stock, making them just a bit thicker and wider than the blades. Four-ply card, he told me. This was a thin card we used for innumerable tasks in the department, about the thickness of four pieces of paper glued together.

I cut out four pieces, tracing around my blades so that the handles would extend about one-thirty-second of an inch beyond the metal and an inch and a half shorter than the cutting edge. I glued these to the blades with PVA, clamping them tight in the press until dry.

This left a tiny gap running around the edges of the handles where the card extended past the blade. To fill this in, I found a piece of linen sewing thread the same thickness as the gap and glued it between the two pieces of card. I repeated this process to make covers to protect the blades from nicking, except that I glued the thread between the two pieces of card without gluing the card to the blades. This way the covers would slide easily on and off the lifting knives.

Next I prepared leather to cover the handles and protective covers for the knives. When I needed to pare down thinly a piece of leather larger than, say, four inches wide, I would use my woodworker's spokeshave. Its blade and base had been angled back, adapting them to leatherwork, and I would scarf off leather until the piece was uniformly thin.

To pare a strip of leather less than four inches wide, I used the Shar-Fix, a wonderful machine that Bill kept in a box in the bottom drawer of his filing cabinet. This was a German machine—an amalgam of clamps, roller, and razor blade— that could pare a strip of leather so thin you could see through it. The leather was clamped between the edge of the razor blade and a roller and, as it was pulled through, thin strips peeled off the suede side. It took only a few minutes to accomplish what would have taken much longer—and been more difficult— with the spokeshave. I clamped the Shar-Fix to my bench, put on my work apron to catch the leather parings in my lap, and adjusted the height of the razor blade to pare very thinly.

I had found two nice pieces of royal blue leather in the scrap box. I was working with goatskin, about one-sixteenth of an inch thick, so I set the razor blade to pare it almost paper thin, hoping that I would be able to pull the leather strip through just once and scarf it as thin as I wanted to. But the first time I pulled one of the strips through, the razor blade bounced and ripped the piece of leather—probably because I tried to pare off too much at once. I raised the blade slightly and tried again on another section of the same strip. This time the machine took off a clean strip of suede. I ran the leather through three times, each time paring it a little thinner. This technique worked well, and after about fifteen minutes, I had two thin pieces of leather and a lap full of suede scraps.

○ ○ ○

> The relationship of a *shokunin* to his tools is . . . very close, for it is through the tools that the work of the *shokunin* is created. Each of the *shokunin*'s tools is his life and pride. (viii)

My favorite tool to watch Bill use was his English paring knife. I appreciated it because of its simplicity and how well it performed—even when I used it. I coveted that knife.

My English paring knife had a steel blade with a soft angle of about twenty degrees on one end. There are also French paring knives that have a blade with a curved end that is sharp all along the curve. Some binders prefer them, but I like having a blade that is sharp only on one side. It's just a matter of preference.

The other end of his knife was mounted into a narrow wooden handle that had been wrapped with a thinly pared strip of black leather that extended up, wrapping the lower part of the blade as well as the handle. Inside Bill's drawer it wore a protective slipcase of board covered by a soft pastel handmade paper that fit down over the cutting edge. All of Bill's best knives had these covers to protect them as they were jostled in the tool drawers, and as I finished mine, they did too.

Such knives are used to edge-pare the leather to put on the spines or covers of books. But paring a supple material like leather around the edges is difficult. Very soft leathers like calf stretch as you pare them and can be difficult to work with. Stiffer leathers like alum-tawed pigskin pare much more easily because they are harder and don't move out from under the blade. But they also can tear more easily because there is less give in the skin. I always preferred goatskin, the middle ground, for paring. It had tricky spots—especially if I needed to use the thicker section of leather that had once covered the spine of the goat—but I learned to pare goat first and always had an affinity for it. For most conservation backings and rebinding, however, we used calf to match what had been on the books originally.

Before you can pare a piece of leather, it is necessary to fasten it down so that you have control over it. The surface the leather is placed on must be hard, yet allow the spokeshave to glide over it. The binders I know all use old lithographic stones for this. The litho stone sits on the edge of your workbench, and the leather is held down by means of a C-clamp that has a piece of wood about the size of a postcard glued to the clamp. You clamp down part of the leather and pare the rest.

To edge-pare a piece of leather, you must run the knife along the edge of the leather, scarfing off a thin strip from the wrong side. Done properly: one sweep of the knife to the right, paring the right three fourths of the strip; one short sweep to the left, finishing up. Result: an evenly pared edge where the leather is uniformly thin. Done badly: many short scarfs to the right; fewer to the left. Result: an unevenly pared edge with thick and thin spots. Or so much stretching of the leather that it ruffles. It's the difference between peeling an apple so that the skin comes off in one or two curls and scraping it off in little bits.

When I began to reback books and edge-pare leather for new spines, I was very, very bad at it. By the time I was finished with my strip of leather, which had started out the size of a business envelope, it would be the size of a movie ticket. The blade of my paring knife felt clumsy in my hand, like neither one of us was sure what to do next. Sometimes the blade would catch in the paring motion and rip the leather, forcing me to get a new piece and start over. The *kan* of paring leather was much harder for me to grasp than the *kan* of papermaking.

The first book I had to reback in leather was a trial. I had my own paring knife at this time and was bravely trying to edge-pare a strip of brown calf. Time after time, I ruined the leather. I watched Bill use his paring knife, mimicking the exact way he held the blade and the motion he made with his hand: smoothly, left to right; right to left. Then I would go back to my bench and try it again. I quickly learned this was one of the training patterns for me as an apprentice: I watched Bill do something; I tried it myself; I did it wrong. I watched Bill do it again, asking questions of him; I tried it again; I did it right.

Sometimes I learned more quickly than others with less direct coaching from Bill. Other times I had to go back to him again and again for guidance. He never once seemed annoyed by my questions or the interruptions I must have caused in his own work. Often if I was having difficulty with a procedure, I would ask Larry's help. Bill occasionally forgot what it was like to learn a bookbinding technique for the first time. Since Larry was closer to my level of experience, he could often spot the problem I was having and tell me how to fix it. He was as patient and kind with me as Bill was.

Sometimes doing something correctly the first time set me up for problems later. While still taking Bill's night class, I made a drop-spine box (also called a clam-shell box) for a Windhover Press book belonging to my mother. Since Bill had bound the edition for Windhover after coming to Iowa, I was able to make the box using the same cloth that was on the cover of the volume. Bill led me carefully through the steps to make the box—measuring the book, cutting the boards and assembling the trays, covering them with paper and cloth, and assembling the box—and it turned out perfectly the first time. The book fit securely into the bottom tray, the box closed securely around it, and it matched the book beautifully. I was impressed. My mother was impressed.

Several months into my apprenticeship, Bill asked me to make a drop-spine box for a book I was treating. I think since the first box had gone so well, both of us thought I would have no problem the second time. I cut out, assembled, and covered *five* sets of trays for that second box before the book fit them correctly. Bill didn't understand exactly which steps were giving me trouble, and I couldn't understand where my *kan* of boxmaking had gone. I labored through several more drop-spine boxes before I realized that I had never had the *kan* of boxmaking in the first place—only beginner's luck.

To get to the sink, counter, and back work areas, Bill had to walk past all our benches. Often he would stop and look over my shoulder, sometimes offering comments on what I was doing, sometimes pausing to demonstrate something that made my work better, easier. When he saw me struggling with my paring knife and yet another piece of brown calf, he stopped at once. He hadn't examined it closely before. Taking my place at the paring stone, Bill tried to pare the leather. His usual smooth motion to the right wasn't so smooth. He stopped and ran his thumb along the edge of my blade.

"Your knife isn't sharp enough. You're tearing the leather strip off rather than slicing it off cleanly."

As I stood looking at my blade that I'd spent days honing, Bill went down to his bench, pulled out his paring knife, and came back to me. With eight simple motions, he pared the leather spine and then handed me his blade. With my thumb,

I could feel the sharp, clean edge on his knife and the dull edge on my own.

"You've been rocking your blade edge ever so slightly on the stones while you sharpen them." As he explained, his hands demonstrated the motions in the air between us. "That rounds the cutting edge and you can't get a clean cut.

"Put this piece of leather on your book, and then work on getting a sharp edge on your knife," Bill said, smiling. "Once you learn how to get that edge on your blade, you'll always know how."

○ ○ ○

Though the urge to add decoration to a tool can express the love of a *shokunin* for the tool, today vendors and manufacturers often prefer to emphasize looks without love and pride, thinking only of profit. I do not think this is a good trend, for the true purpose of a tool is to be productive, not pretty. (182)

The next step was to cover the handles and blade covers of my lifting knives with leather. With a small whisk, I stirred some wheat paste into some tap water in a bowl until it was as thick as cream. While it thickened for a few minutes, I trimmed down some pieces of blue goatskin. I needed four strips that conformed in shape to the handles and covers, each wide enough to wrap all the way around each handle or cover, the edges overlapping slightly on one side. I pared these edges even thinner with my paring knife so that they could overlap without a noticeable ridge. I was very good at paring bits of leather that didn't go on books.

With cotton, I dampened the first piece with some water on the right side and glued it out. This moisture kept the paste from drying too quickly and made the leather more supple to work with. I placed the leather on one side of the handle and wrapped it around, the pared edges overlapping as I'd planned. I had to be very careful as I handled the strip because wet leather stretches very easily. I rubbed it down gently with my bone folder, smoothing the leather into place around the bottom curve of the handle. With the other lifting knife, I carefully tucked the edge of the leather closest to the cutting edge under the card the tiniest bit so that there wouldn't be an unfinished edge. Then I placed the knife between blotters to dry. I repeated this process for the other handle and covers, drying the covers on the knives themselves so they would keep their size and shape.

When I had first begun wrapping the handles of my tools and making their blade covers, I had decided that I wanted to put some mark on them that would distinguish them from everyone else's—something to show they were mine. I had wrapped the handle of my spokeshave in alternating strips of bright blue and light gray leather. The handle and blade cover of my French paring knife were covered in black goatskin. In the handle I'd onlaid a thin blue leather lightning bolt, symbolic of the blade's ability to move quickly.

It was autumn when I made my lifting knives, and leaves were falling off the trees outside the department's windows.

When I pared the blue leather for them, I had also run a tiny scrap of green and a tiny scrap of deep red leather through the Shar-Fix. With these I cut out four leaves: the red, oak leaves; the green, more generic leaf shapes. After the leather of the new handles of my lifting knives were dry, I carefully dampened a spot on both sides of each and, with paste, onlaid the leaves. With the tip of my smallest bone folder, I incised veins into the leaves and put the knives under light weight to dry. I had worked hard on the lifting knives—the first tools I had made completely myself—and I wanted them to be special.

○ ○ ○

During my apprenticeship, it was common for my master, an impatient man, to correct me when I made a mistake by hitting me with whatever was at hand (often a hammer). Now, as I look back, these incidents strike me as having great symbolic value. An apprentice, after all, is like a hot iron, needing to be shaped . . . by the hands and tools of the master. (59)

The apprentices that Bill took in Iowa were very fortunate. Since he was working for the university, he didn't have to worry about such things as money for upkeep or new supplies, or about keeping on schedule with jobs for clients. Our only client was the University of Iowa Libraries' Special Collections. Books arrived in the department from the rare book rooms in the Main Library, Hardin Library for the Health Sciences, and occasionally from the art and music libraries. We never repaired materials from the circulating collection; a separate department in the library handled those. I had many friends who worked in conservation units at other libraries where they had to take care of the circulating material as well. That takes up so much of their time, they rarely get to work on the special collection items.

Bill said that not having the worries of running a business allowed him great freedom with us. He could take the time to teach us things slowly and not have to worry about deadlines. We were not under pressure to produce skilled work and income. It was a situation that made everyone happy.

Occasionally someone from Special Collections would come down to our department to find out what had happened to a volume we'd had for a long time—usually in response to a request for the book from a library patron. But although we felt no sense of urgency to finish things quickly, Bill liked us to stay busy and keep work moving in and out of the department.

Often Bill told us stories of conservators and book-binders he knew or had worked with. These stories usually came up in response to specific situations and served as an instructional tool—usually emphasizing things we shouldn't do. I loved hearing these stories and felt a strong sense of connection with the struggles of the binders and conservators who had gone before me. One of Bill's former apprentices told me once, "You have to make three thousand mistakes before you can be a good bookbinder."

When one of us complained about how long it was taking to mend the pages of an entire book, Bill would tell the story of a conservator he knew who worked in one of America's most prestigious conservation labs. This person was so meticulous about his mending—teasing the small strips of mending paper into minute pieces to mend pages almost invisibly—that it took him forever to finish one book. His supervisor would finally get fed up with him and take the book away, giving it to someone else to finish. By comparison, our mending went quickly.

When someone was learning to sew a text block together for the first time, the question always came up about how long to cut the piece of sewing thread. If you ran out of thread before you finished, it was necessary to tie on another, using a weaver's knot to hold it fast. This knot is not particularly difficult to tie, but beginners always seemed to prefer not to tie on more thread—as if to do so was a sign of ineptness.

At this point, Bill liked to tell the story of one of his apprentices who hated to tie on new pieces of sewing thread. He would figure out how much thread he needed to sew a volume and carefully measure out an incredibly long piece of thread with which he then sewed the book. Bill would describe how once the piece of thread was so long, it ran the entire length of the shop in Chicago, pointing out that to keep such a long piece of thread untangled and free of knots while sewing took far longer than tying on a new piece. I was never sure whether or not to believe this story, but after getting tied up myself in long pieces of thread a few times, I too learned the weaver's knot.

When I learned to wash paper, Bill told me the story of a young conservator who washed a manuscript without testing the ink for water-solubility. She carefully placed the document in a wash tray with deionized water, but when she checked on it later, the words had all washed away. He looked at me at this point in the story, and said, "She didn't last long as a conservator." I found this story horrifying and imagined this woman, in disgrace, driving a taxicab somewhere. I never washed a manuscript document without thinking of her, and I never forget to test for water-solubility.

The most comforting story was the one Bill invariably told when someone made a mistake while blind tooling leather on the cover of a book. This treacherous process of tooling involves stamping an impression in damp leather with a heated brass tool. Not only are you using a tool that is difficult to place correctly with its tiny letter of the alphabet mounted on one end, you are also using it while it is hot. Many things can go wrong along the way.

Early in my training, I dropped a heated tool onto the cover of a book in the wrong spot, leaving a mark on the leather. Bill helped me work over the spot with a damp piece of cotton—a "mouse," he called it. The moisture fluffed the leather back up, removing the mark almost completely.

He then went up to the shelves next to his desk, ruffled through some papers, and came back with a color photograph showing the front of a tooled book. It was covered in a soft brown leather and had been bound by George Baer, a man

Bill had worked with at the Cuneo Press in Chicago when he first moved to the United States. The front of the book was tooled elaborately with the top portion of a sheaf of wheat. Bill pointed to a lower corner of the pictured binding. I noticed that there was a tiny fly tooled into the cover design.

"See that fly?" Bill asked. "When George originally designed this binding, there was no fly. In the process of tooling the leather he dropped one of his hot tools into the soft leather. Since he couldn't remove the mark without water staining this type of leather, he turned it into this tiny fly. Very few people know that this fly was never meant to be there." He smiled at me. "There's always a way to fix a mistake."

I heard Bill tell these stories over and over to instruct, warn, or comfort. Later, when I began to teach bookbinding myself and to help train new apprentices, I told them, too. The photograph of the book with the fly tooled into the design always remained accessible on the shelf to show to others. I occasionally went back to look at it again myself.

INITIATION

Oyster knife

A photograph taken on the morning of July 1, 1987, shows me standing in my kitchen, my blue tackle box in one hand and my brown sack lunch in the other. I am smiling in this grown-up version of a child's first day of school snapshot. I am on my way out the door to my first day as an apprentice, and I can hardly wait to get there.

Bill was out of town on vacation.

Larry gave me ten books that Bill had set aside for me to repair. Ten books that I had no idea what to do with. Almost all of my work in Bill's classes for two and a half years had been making historical models or learning simple bindings. I had never worked on a book needing conservation treatment.

The first books I had to work on dated from roughly the first half of the twentieth century, except for one book from the eighteenth century. They ranged from a single-section Dada pamphlet to a large perfect-bound art book of heavy glazed paper. Two had text blocks that had pulled free from their cloth and paper covers. Two leather-bound volumes, both editions of William Blake's *Songs of Innocence,* were made up of heavy single sheets that had been glued along one edge. Their pages were pulling loose from the covers. Four art books—one, a volume of Blake's sketches—needed the protective enclosures repaired for their accompanying plates or minor work done on their text blocks (such as cutting open the pages). The Dada pamphlet and eighteenth-century book of letters both needed full conservation treatments.

From what I observed, Bill liked to have his apprentices and students begin working on newer material from the nineteenth and twentieth centuries. He slowly moved us back through binding history to work on older, more valuable books as we acquired knowledge and confidence in our abilities.

I was glad Bill had started me out with books that were relatively new. There was a wide range of problems to be treated, and I wasn't afraid of ruining anything that was irreplaceable. I knew from classes I had taken in graduate school that there were plenty of copies of Blake's works around, so they didn't intimidate me.

Bill had told me before I started my apprenticeship that the grant under which I was employed from the National Endowment for the Arts required that I provide a yearly report to include photographs of books I had treated. He wanted me to take before and after slides of everything I worked on. That seemed odd to me at the time. Bill only took photographs of of his fine bindings or things he was going to give public lectures about, or that were of great historical importance, such as one of the Audubon *Birds of America*. Other apprentices only took slides sporadically. But I was glad to begin accompanied by a photographic record. It appealed to my methodical sense of how things should be done.

To that photographic record, I added my own set of meticulous notes documenting my work on each volume. That way I had material to refer to on how I had treated a particular problem. They later provided a useful reference when treating books with similar problems.

Besides my work notes, I tried to keep a journal of my experiences in the department. I felt privileged to have been selected as Bill's first female apprentice. I knew this was a part of my life that I would always want to remember. Writing it down seemed the best way to hold on to the terrors and successes of learning a handcraft. I kept a journal fairly regularly for the first nine months. It records in detail the five weeks it took me to finish the work required on those first ten volumes.

○ ○ ○

7/1/87 – The end of my first day on the job and everyone else has gone home. I am in charge of locking up without setting off the alarms, trusting I remember how to set them. It was a very long day. And this stool is so hard.

7/7/87 – I have learned that to move with any speed at all is to make mistakes. I tried to take the mull and spine lining off a copy of Blake's sketches, accidentally pulled out the threads and tapes, and as a result, will now have to pull and resew the whole book.

7/8/87 – I finished my first book today. It was just a simple one-signature Dada pamphlet in a paper cover, but I washed and deacidified it, repaired the cover with kozo, and put it all back together. I am so pleased with it.

7/9/87 – I have discovered that I ask two different kinds of questions. The first I ask not knowing how to do something and wanting directions. The second I ask when I'm pretty sure I know how to do something and I want an answer that confirms it.

Another thing I've noticed is that one benefit of having other people around is that there's always someone who can help you figure out how to do something. Or who will come along and suggest a better way to do something. In a way, this makes everyone a master and apprentice equally.

7/10/87 – I have lived through my first full week of work. I didn't think I would get through this afternoon. I finally had to go and drink a cup of the horrible black coffee from the urn in the break room. Boy, am I wired now!

○ ○ ○

Once I had begun working in the Conservation Department as a full-time apprentice, I discovered my new job required initiation into a number of aspects of learning. First, as the newest employee in the department, I had to observe and fit into the daily routine.

Second, I had to master a full-time job. I had never spent eight consecutive hours a day at the same task. My day had always been broken up in segments: some time spent in class, some time spent teaching, some time spent doing daily chores. Now I had to develop a more concentrated form of studying: how to learn something by watching and doing, by performing and producing simultaneously while working with one teacher on a concentrated basis, and to learn how to pace my work throughout the day.

Third, I also had to define for myself what apprenticeship in general was, and what mine would embrace specifically. Bill never discussed with me precisely what my apprenticeship would include, nor was there a job description, even though I was technically an employee of the university. What was his role as my teacher?

First came initiation into the daily routine.

I noticed quickly once I had begun my apprenticeship that the days had a set pattern. Bill would arrive promptly at 8:00 A.M. and walk quickly across the department to the corner of the room with his desk, bench, and filing cabinet. He would place his battered leather briefcase on his chair, take out his sandwich (always wrapped in foil) and a piece of fruit (usually a banana), and lay them on top of the filing cabinet next to his cup. Then he would run his fingers once through his hair, red-gone-to-gray, and walk the length of the room to

Larry's bench next to mine to talk for a few minutes.

The conversation centered on the evening or weekend just passed. Bill would tell about the round of golf he had played the evening before. Or the racquetball game. How after dinner he and his wife, Bernie, had driven out to Kent Park and walked their dog, Toby, around the lake. About how Toby had bounded away from Bill and run straight into the water. How he had gotten scolded by Bernie because the dog got all wet.

Larry would counter with details about how his dog, Lucy, was fairing: failing eyesight, trouble getting off and on the front porch. With what he was doing in his garden. How he was moving three hundred red tulip bulbs because it was time to. I would stand at my bench, occasionally contributing, always listening. I had cats and only a few dozen flower bulbs in my yard that stayed put where they'd been planted.

Sometimes (actually, it got to be quite often after awhile) I would arrive a bit late. Bill would already be standing next to Larry's bench discussing a book he had just read. Or complaining that Bernie had made him toast that morning for breakfast instead of pancakes (she *always* made him pancakes). I would walk back to my bench and Bill and Larry would greet me cheerfully and ask about my weekend or evening. I would stop to chat. That way I felt as if I had joined the conversation instead of just hovering nearby. After fifteen minutes or so, Bill would return to his bench and we would all get to work.

The Conservation Department is on the first floor of the Main Library tucked between the employees' break room and the library administration offices, its windows facing Madison Street and the Engineering Building. At the time I started my apprenticeship, it was a long, L-shaped work space with six benches along the windows and two more in the short leg of the L. Equipment and work areas were spread throughout the space.

I had made sure I had gotten a bench facing the windows so that I would have good light and be able to look outside. Larry's bench was perpendicular to mine and he worked facing me. Bill was two benches away. If I had a question, I turned and asked Larry. I was shy at first about bothering Bill.

Sometimes the radio on the corner of Bill's bench would be turned softly to a classical music station. We would work away the morning with Bach and Mozart floating around the room. As a result, I have always associated bookbinding and conservation work with classical music, and not with the rock and roll, folk music, or National Public Radio that some of my coworkers in the department preferred.

I was always enthusiastic about starting in on the day's work. Except for days when classes were taught in the department after hours, I always left my next morning's work laid out on my bench when I left each day. This answered the question about where to start and helped me to focus first thing in the morning. The morning hours passed quickly.

At 10:15 or so, Bill would put down what he was working

with, take up his cup, and walk around the corner into the library employees' break room. For fifteen minutes he would sit and have coffee, again describing Toby's latest antics and picking up the latest library gossip. Then he would come back, return his cup to the top of the filing cabinet, and go right back to work. He repeated the same procedure at 3:15 in the afternoon. I always took breaks as well, although mine were erratically timed. Larry almost never took a break, except on those occasions when we all took one together for some reason.

I would often take a book into the break room to read while I had a cup of tea. In the beginning, I knew almost no one on the library staff, and I felt better reading, my head in my book, than sitting among strangers in one of the arranged groups of couches. If Bill was still there, I never presumed to sit with him, but I could hear his warm laugh from wherever I was.

Other times I would go and look up books in the card catalogue and search for them among the stacks. From the very beginning, I was interested in the notion of apprenticeship and what exactly it was I had committed myself to do, so those searches were for books dealing with apprenticeship. I knew about medieval craft apprenticeships from my graduate studies in the history of the book. There were a few books in the library about apprenticeship and industrialization; none contained information about the specific history of bookbinding apprenticeships.

One of the first things Bill had given me after I had agreed to become his apprentice was a membership form to the Guild of Book Workers. It was a national organization of hand bookbinders, illuminators, calligraphers, decorated papermakers, and book restorers founded in 1906 to establish a feeling of kinship and mutual interest among workers in the hand book crafts. Over the years, the guild's membership grew to include conservators, papermakers, printers, and others dedicated to the book arts. It publishes a newsletter and journal, maintains a national membership, and supports nine regional chapters. Once a year, the members meet for the annual Standards of Excellence Seminar at which four members demonstrate techniques and discuss how to attain excellence in the book arts. I quickly realized, however, that this guild was nothing like the guilds of the Middle Ages, and I continued to search out information on apprenticeship.

Lunch was at noon. Bill would eat his sandwich and banana in the break room and then go uptown or do private work in the department. After he and Bernie moved within walking distance of the library, he would sometimes go home for lunch. Larry and I would usually sit in the break room to read and eat. Larry would go back in the department and do conservation work for private clients, but I almost always left the building.

I would walk uptown to the shops to run errands. Now that I was working forty hours a week, I had little time to go shopping and do other chores. A sixty-minute lunch hour always seemed rushed—especially in that first Christmas season. Plus, I had to get some fresh air. The Main Library was not known for its accurate temperature control or efficient air circulation.

Afternoons in the Conservation Department were much like the mornings: full of quiet work. Once school started in the fall, two work-study students began working afternoons. One was Bill's youngest daughter, Lisa. The other was Sally Key, who was finishing her degree in library science and who later became Bill's second female apprentice. Sally and Lisa made afternoons in the department much noisier. They were good friends, having both worked together the previous semester. Sally and I knew each other from when we had taken papermaking together the year before.

Bill enjoyed the clamor to a point. Sometimes he got after us for talking too much. Or in Lisa's and Sally's cases, laughing too loudly. Bill was serious about the work and we were expected to be also. I came to cherish the morning hours; they were quieter. I found it easier to concentrate then and to ask Bill questions without interruptions.

Such a set schedule had disadvantages. By four o'clock every afternoon, I was almost crazy to get out of the building. My wooden stool had no back rest, and by then I longed for a deep sofa to sink into and a coffee table to put my feet up on. Enthusiasm for the day's work had faded. Quickly I learned to save the piles of reading material—bookbinding and conservation journals we passed through the department—for those late afternoon hours when I could no longer concentrate on handwork. I also used that time to read books from the shelf next to Bill's desk about binding history and to write in my journal and catch up on my work notes. The apprenticeship was very important to me, but I reached a point when my discipline failed, my brain-hand coordination ceased to function, and I just wanted it to be 5:00, when we locked up, cheerfully wished each other good evening, and went home. The hardest part of that job was staying in the same room eight hours a day, five days a week. It never got any easier.

○ ○ ○

7/15/87 – *Yesterday was a very bad day. I was trimming a cloth cover to allow for a new spine to be inserted. I got the cover turned around on the bench and put a slit all along the fore edge! And it was that awful Blake book that I pulled all the stitches out of and had to resew. Fortunately it was the back cover and hopefully it won't show when I'm finished with it. I left grad school to get away from the likes of William Blake!*

It's funny how I take a dislike to certain books and love others. I spent the morning sewing Letters from Edinburgh, *and felt as though I had lavished time on an old friend.*

7/17/87 – *Bonnie Jo Cullison came today from the Newberry Library in Chicago to give a talk on the preservation of library materials. She talked about how "preservation" is concerned with all aspects of protecting a library collection, whereas "conservation" is concerned with the limited aspects of taking care of the books on a more individual basis.*

She talked about the Newberry's policy of keeping the books in separate storage areas from the reading rooms the patrons use: "What is good for people is not good for books." It takes the central focus of the library away from the reader and places it on the book as an archival object. I've never been in a library where I couldn't just wander up and down the stacks of books. We are spoiled by having books around to use whenever we please.

7/20/87 – Bill's back from his vacation today. Still working on the Blake book.

○ ○ ○

There were many aspects of managing my day that I needed to learn—tricks to keeping busy and pacing myself through the procedures I was learning and the books I was treating. Initiation into those lessons came while working on my first ten books.

I began with the Dada pamphlet. It was a single section of pages with a simple stapled paper cover, and I chose to treat it first because there was no leather or cloth to mess with. I carefully took out the rusted staple that held it together. The pages were acidic and needed to be washed, as did the cover. Larry carefully showed me how. It was then, that first morning, that I learned why I had more than one book to work on at a time. While the Dada pamphlet was soaking in the deionized water wash, I had to begin treating something else.

That was one of the lessons that didn't come easily at first: how to juggle several conservation treatments at once. I learned that while one book was washing or being deacidified or drying, I could take apart another volume for treatment. Or mend pages of something already washed, deacidified, and dried. Or work on rebacking a volume in cloth. Or do any one of numerous other tasks required by the volumes I had.

At most stages of treatment there was something wet— either from washing, deacidifying, or gluing—that needed to dry. I came slowly to a pattern of working on one item as far as I could until it needed to dry and then moved on to the next item, working on it as far as I could. The trick I learned was to do this rotating through no more than three items at once. More than that got to be confusing—especially while I was learning new procedures and techniques. In the first batch of books, I also had to be sure I kept the materials for the Blake books separate. It would not have been acceptable to get the pages from the two different editions of *Songs of Innocence* mixed up.

Rotating through work also helped prevent me from becoming bored with one procedure or book. For example, I tended to mend the pages of a book over several days, working on it for a few hours at a time—usually in the morning when I was freshest. Other apprentices had different styles of pacing themselves. Larry often mended an entire book from beginning to end, mending all day, for several days if necessary. I didn't have his stamina and focus, and preferred to break up the routine of what I did each day. Bill didn't seem to care how we paced the books we worked on as long as there was progress toward their completion.

When we finished a treatment, we briefly wrote up what we had done. Bill copied this from our notes onto the small card that was tipped with a little paste into the back cover of the volume or into its protective enclosure, if it had one. I didn't trust my memory for details of conservation treatments and made out a form on an 8½-by-11-inch sheet of paper that I could use to keep track of my work. Other apprentices had bound blank books for recording their treatments, but I found small, bound pages confining. My larger sheets gave me lots of room for notes and drawings, and it made compiling brief details for the treatment reports easier.

After Bill saw and used my notes on my books, filled out in my tiny neat printing, he stopped condensing them for the treatment reports and gave me a stack of the small sheets to fill out myself. It became a department policy then that the apprentices and student workers filled out their own cards instead of having Bill copy their notes. It saved him time and became a more accurate record of who had treated the book. When Bill had written up the cards, he had always put his own initials at the end (perhaps to signify that he had checked the book over before it went back to Special Collections). Once we started filling out the cards ourselves, we put our own initials at the end to show who had performed the treatment.

I also learned that it was very important to keep track of all the pieces of books as they were pulled apart for treatment. Unnumbered pages of volumes were numbered by hand in pencil to facilitate collating them in the correct order. Cover pieces were carefully kept in one envelope or pile on my bench so that I didn't misplace them. After I mislabeled the first British books I worked on, I always drew careful diagrams of things I took off and had to replace to avoid repeating that mistake.

That autumn, Sally was working on a complicated treatment of two anatomical broadsides done by Jean Ruel in 1539. In a lift-the-flap approach, the male and female figures had printed paper layers you could lift to see their internal organs, including a tiny fetus in the female. Sally had to carefully remove each flap while diagramming its placement, and wash, deacidify, mend, and replace them. These items were extremely valuable and belonged to the John Martin Rare Book Room in the Hardin Library for the Health Sciences. Sally was very careful every step of the way.

During the reassembly of the man, she discovered his kidneys were missing. She searched for them. The rest of us searched for them. We looked everywhere over and over again, knowing the gentleman wouldn't function quite so well or be as valuable without his kidneys. That Saturday, I went in to Conservation to make up some extra hours and discovered Sally already there searching some more. She had to find the kidneys before Bill came back on Monday from a conference. In the process of my own work, I went to use one of the small book presses and discovered the kidneys neatly resting between two blotters, where they had been placed to flatten gently before being reattached. Bill never knew about the missing kidneys, and we were reminded to keep careful track of the pieces we were working with.

At first, I needed a great deal of direction about how to plan my work day. I was completely ignorant of conservation techniques, and although I understood simple book construction, I was unfamiliar with a lot of the materials and supplies in the shop. I had to ask about every step before I did it, every material before I used it. I'm sure I was a nuisance. Sometimes I wondered if Bill had planned his vacation for my first two weeks on purpose. But Larry was very patient with me and tireless with his explanations and demonstrations. I was to remember that later when it came my turn to help initiate new apprentices into the ways of the department.

When I began my apprenticeship with Bill, I had twenty-four years of classroom learning behind me. Twenty-four years of having teachers stand in front of a room and talk to me, lecture me, guide me in my readings and writings. I was told what to do and how to do it, but for the most part, not shown. For my efforts I earned a master's degree in English literature.

At that point, I had also spent five years teaching others, working as a freshman composition teacher in two different universities. I took on the role of the teacher telling her students how to read and write.

But when I got my master's degree, the term had no real meaning for me. I did not consider myself a "master" of the areas of English literature I had studied. I felt comfortable teaching writing because I wrote a lot myself and felt able to describe to my students my own techniques and those recommended by others. I also loved to read and could share this. I had a lot to offer with good feedback to my students—I was a close reader. But I was not a "master" of reading and writing.

When I began studying with Bill, I had also had more than four years of experience in bookbinding, having worked for the Silver Spring Bindery, as well as taking Bill's night classes. I had overseen the binding of three volumes of poetry while I worked at Windhover Press for Kim Merker. I had a good idea of how simple case bindings (hardcover books) were constructed, but lacked any type of finesse with the tools and materials. I also had some bad work habits, although I didn't realize it at the time. Bill once said to me that the best new apprentices were those with no previous binding experience and therefore no bad habits.

Early in my apprenticeship, I was constructing a new hard cover for a book. I had cut out a large rectangle of book cloth, glued down the spine stiffener and two pieces of board that would be the front and back covers, and was busy folding over the excess border of cloth to the inside of the cover. Bill, on his way back to the sink to wash a glue brush, walked past my bench just as I—with a final flourish—turned the new cover in my hands and banged down two of the fore edge corners of the cover with my bone folder. Bill was instantly at my side.

"What are you doing?" he asked as I turned the book around, preparing to bang the two remaining corners. I stopped, realizing by his tone that I was doing something wrong.

"Whenever I made covers at Silver Spring, we always knocked the sharp points off the corners with our bone folders." I replied, still holding the cover suspended in midair.

"Why?" he persisted.

"I was told it was because the corners would get bumped, and this way we had already rounded the point." I put the cover down on my bench.

"We do not 'bang the corners' off new covers," he stated. "If the point seems too sharp, round it gently with your bone folder, but do not 'bang it.'" He continued on to the sink to wash out his brush.

Having been a student for so long, I also brought along habits of learning that I never got rid of. Twenty-four years in the classroom had made me a chronic notetaker. It was built into my way of learning something, and I couldn't give it up.

Bill didn't approve of my note-taking. He kept no notes of his own, and I think he considered it a waste of time. But he had learned bookbinding in a tradition where he repeated procedures over and over again in a production setting—

perhaps hundreds of times. I'm sure that made him less likely to forget the things he knew. As a journeyman binder in England, he had worked for a number of firms that specialized in different types of bookbinding—such as F. G. Marshall of Surrey, which produced books of remembrance (one-of-a-kind bindings done of letters memorializing someone who has died). After working at one place and mastering its type of binding, he moved on to work elsewhere, in the journeyman tradition.

Bill and I came from different backgrounds and had different approaches to learning and mastering a process. I would execute several cloth spine rebackings in a row and then not do one again for several months. Having my notes to review helped me remember the procedure quickly and correctly when I was called on to reback a book again. After a period of time, I repeated some procedures enough to no longer need my notes. Others—like how to take the measurements for a drop-spine box—I always referred to because it saved me the time of having to refigure the steps each time I made the protective enclosure for different-sized books.

Some apprentices wrote things down in a detailed manner like I did. Others never recorded any procedures, swayed by Bill's emphasis on doing, not writing. I took down directions from techniques he taught me directly. I also took notes on information from binding video tapes, lectures, and workshops. I wrote things down on loose-leaf paper, drew diagrams in the margins, and filed them in ring binders according to topic.

After Bill died, I was very glad I had those notes. They were parts of his instruction I might have otherwise forgotten.

I think Bill was afraid my note-taking would convince me there was only one way to approach each type of treatment. But I quickly learned each book was unique and had different problems that had to be handled in individual ways. Rebacking a cloth or leather book often follows many of the same steps, but they have to be adapted to the particular style and construction of each volume. Those general steps of technique were what I recorded.

Bill got after me in the beginning for my scribbling.

"Don't take notes. Just watch me do this. You learn by doing, not by writing." I would carefully watch his demonstration, go back to my bench and repeat the procedure, and then write out my notes. Or I would listen to his directions, jot them down briefly, and then follow them, later recording the process in greater detail. This was especially helpful when procedures took several hours or several days. Even though Bill was always very patient with me, I didn't want to keep asking him to repeat directions. It didn't seem to be an efficient use of our time together. In the end, Bill just ignored my note-taking.

○ ○ ○

7/21/87 – Today was the best day of work so far. I felt like I was able to pace myself and I got quite a lot done.

Blake finally got put into his cover and nothing went too terribly wrong. I wish the books I'm working on could speak. I'd like to know who tore their covers or spilled on their pages.

7/22/87 — Went to peel down the blue paper cover on the spine edge of the boards of Letters *to insert a stronger cloth spine cover, and found that there was an exact duplicate of the top cover underneath it. It makes me feel good that back in 1776, someone didn't put the cover on right the first time. Of course, he didn't do it much better the second time! I wonder if someone will undo one of the books I'm restoring 200 years from now and wonder about me.*

7/23/87 — I finished three books today! That makes four out of my first ten. It's so nice when it all comes together at the end. I think Bill has been pleased with the books I have finished so far. I know I have been.

7/24/87 — Put the original cloth spine back on top of the new cloth spine of the Blake book today. I thought it looked great until Bill told me I had it on upside down. It seems that the British title the spines of their books from the bottom reading up instead of from the top reading down. I had to carefully peel it up with my lifting knives and reattach it. For once and for all, I thoroughly detest William Blake!

7/27/87 – *The days are getting easier although I fear Monday mornings will always be difficult as far as getting up and out the door on time.*

Had to undo another mistake today. I glued down the hinges of a book in rather a mess. Turns out it was because the spine of the book is too wide and I will have to case the book in a different manner. That's one of the ways this apprenticeship system works so well. When I mess something up, Bill can tell me why. I've learned a great deal from my mistakes. Sometimes it's more beneficial to do things wrong in terms of knowledge gained.

8/4/87 – *Finished my first ten books yesterday. They sit piled up on the corner of my bench. I am loath to surrender them to Bill and Special Collections. Too bad I don't get to keep the books I work on. One of the student workers seems to feel the same way. She kept some of the books she'd treated on her bench so long that Bill finally got after her to send them back to Special Collections. He was afraid they were getting damaged from the sunlight coming in the windows.*

8/11/87 – *Today I got two trays finished for my next box and sewed Whitman. I am writing down Bill's way of making a box and, with diagramming, the whole process takes longer.*

8/13/87 – Got a new book to do today (another edition of Leaves of Grass). *This is the second most valuable one in the library's Whitman collection. I feel a little awed by that fact, but honored Bill has given it to me.*

○ ○ ○

Historically, apprenticeship has been training in a craft or trade in which a student learns from someone who is considered a master in this area. A legal contract between them defined the duration and conditions of their relationship. Since this type of learning was well suited to domestic industries in which the master operated on his premises, apprentices usually lived with him, creating an extended family relationship. Apprentices often married into the master's family, making this relationship permanent.

In the thirteenth century, craft guilds emerged in Western Europe as a way to supervise the quality and methods of production. They regulated the conditions of employment between masters and apprentices and didn't let a master take on more employees than he could train effectively. After an apprentice had completed the full term of his training—usually seven years—and had demonstrated his ability by examination or by completion of a masterpiece, he was considered a master craftsman. Sometimes after completion of the apprenticeship, he might work for daily wages as a journeyman to receive further training.

Although I had a verbal employment agreement with Bill, he never discussed the specific details with me before I began—neither what I had to do under the terms of the NEA grant, which had been obtained and was renewed each year by the library, beyond the yearly report, nor what he planned to teach me or expected me to learn. From what I knew of his previous apprentices, Bill favored apprenticeships of five to seven years, terminated when he and the apprentice felt satisfied the training was complete—and when the apprentice had a job to move on to. He trained them in conservation procedures, and also in edition and fine binding—taking a text block and putting a more elaborate binding on it, usually of decorated leather.

Bill and I did have one unique agreement when I began my apprenticeship: I did not have to do any of the edition binding work that came into the department from Windhover Press. For two and a half years I had worked for an Iowa City edition binder, Silver Spring. While I had worked as the printing assistant at Windhover, I had also done three editions of bindings—one completely by myself, and two with the help of other students at the press. I was sick of doing bindings in batches of two hundred and fifty. Bill agreed that I had a good grasp of what goes into edition binding and excused me from having to do any more. He did tell me that he wanted me to do one fine binding a year while I worked for him. I think this was because he had come to conservation after learning production binding and doing fine one-of-a-kind bindings such as he had done while he worked for the John F. Cuneo Company in Chicago, and he wanted his apprentices to know all sides of the craft. Gradually I came to see that there were many other aspects to my training.

Since coming to Iowa, Bill had also become interested in doing models of historical binding styles. He did one-of-a-kind binding replicas such as that of the Stoneyhurst Gospel (a seventh-century manuscript of the Gospel of St. John that is the oldest European book to have survived in its original binding), as well as models typical of certain styles of binding throughout the centuries. He began the department's collection of historical bindings with the help of Mark Esser, the apprentice who came with Bill from Chicago to finish his training. Larry and I also contributed a book each to the collection.

The apprentices were expected to study these models and other bindings and complete some of their own with Bill's guidance. While taking Bill's classes and after my apprenticeship began, I completed four historical models of my own.

I spent most of my time doing conservation treatments. Along with that came my initiation into treatment documentation—before and after slides of my work. Bill, at first, had loaned the department his own camera that he used to take slides of his models and fine bindings. Later Conservation got its own camera. At first, I used two 35 mm cameras my father-in-law had given me. After several months of using them and producing over exposed, off-color, blurry slides, I took them to a camera shop to have them examined. When the owner told me they were only good for boat anchors, I invested in a new camera and lens to do the copy work my job required.

I also learned that part of the problem with the inaccurate coloration of the slides was due to the combination of florescent and incandescent bulbs we used in the Conservation Department: they mingled with the sunlight pouring in through the windows, producing what the man in the camera shop labeled a "witch's brew" of light. Bill purchased photographic lights for the department, and with a new filter, my slides improved one hundred percent. I was quickly learning there was more to conservation work than simply treating books. I became quite expert at taking slides of my books in the departmental setting—a skill, however, I never transferred to photographing live subjects in other settings.

Bill considered education to be an important part of his work—educating the public about what conservation was, teaching new students the elements of binding, and teaching apprentices to carry on the craft. He sometimes ranted about a former apprentice of his who was busy with other aspects of the craft and not taking apprentices or students of his own. Bill considered it a waste if he trained people who then just kept what they knew to themselves. We were expected to teach as our apprenticeships progressed, and to continue teaching afterward.

When I began working in the department, the night bookbinding classes taught through the university's Saturday and Evening Program had progressed from Bill's original class to two. Mark Esser had begun an introductory class in non-adhesive binding to prepare students to take Bill's more advanced class in which students worked on individual projects. Bill was proud of these courses and was glad that we were helping foster an interest in binding. Some of our students from those classes have gone into conservation or bookbinding careers.

A large part of what appealed to me about conservation was the fact that I treated unique items. Repetition had been a drudge in my experiences with letterpress printing and hand papermaking. In book conservation, the techniques were the same but each item required a different approach. It was rarely boring.

There were also aspects of my apprenticeship specific to working in the Main Library—things that Bill's apprentices in Chicago hadn't needed to learn as part of their training. Bill was a member of the Library Exhibition Committee formed in 1987 that had begun regularly installing exhibits of library material. The committee used the display cases in the North Lobby to provide more visibility for the library's resources and collections. It became routine for one apprentice to be assigned to work with the librarians coordinating each exhibit to give them advice about the safest way to display books and other archival items, as well as to help build support stands to keep the books open safely and securely.

As part of our preparation for helping with these exhibits, Bill gave each of us a photocopy of Christopher Clarkson's

Exhibiting Rare Books: A Practical Guide. It was very unusual for him to give us any reading material connected directly with our work, but he felt this guide would provide us with important information on how to care for items on exhibit. Chris, conservator at that time for the Bodleian Library in Oxford, England, was a friend of Bill's with whom I had studied at one of the Paper and Book Intensives, a two-week summer workshop with classes on topics relating to conservation, bookbinding, papermaking, and other book arts. Although the guide was geared toward older books of the fourteenth and fifteenth centuries such as those Chris worked with in the Bodleian, the principles were still applicable to our exhibits of modern books.

○ ○ ○

8/10/87 – What a weekend! I drove to Des Moines Friday afternoon to pick up Amy and Louise at the airport and go to the Marriott Hotel for the Library Binding Service Conference, "The Lessons of History & Experience in the Design of Conservation Bindings." LBS had gotten together a lot of the big names in conservation to give presentations. Bill gave a talk on his nonadhesive binding structures and historical models.

Of course, things promptly broke into the strata of conservators. On the first level are people like Bill—the best conservators who speak at conferences like this one.

On the second level are people who are good enough to be teachers as well as conservators, but who are not quite "masters." They seem to travel in smaller groups of people who studied together and remain friends. Then there are levels of people below who just have jobs as conservators and who fall into groups according to where they work and who they know. Neophytes like Amy and I are way down at the bottom.

Amy and I were watching all these groups circulate for cocktails one evening when we noticed that the second and lower levels only talk to members of their level and others in the higher levels. The people in the first level, like Bill, will talk to and be cordial to everyone. They no longer seem to have their egos tied up in what everyone else thinks of them. We decided that we would remember not to do this when we reach the higher levels. Amy and I continued to watch everyone else, happy when Bill came to talk to us about how we liked the conference.

8/12/87 – Home again and the conference has paid off already. First, I sewed my Whitman with the reinforced link stitch that one of the presenters had spoken about. Then I colored and textured a piece of linen for a spine rebacking using a technique that someone else had demonstrated. It will work on the book much better than a plain dyed cloth would have.

The thing I enjoyed most about the conference was

getting to listen to all those talented people—hear about their work and look at their slides. The one thing I noticed, though, was that all the speakers were men, and only one-fourth of them had been born in this country. We need some strong American women in conservation. Maybe the next few years will change that. Or maybe they're out there and just aren't getting the recognition the men do.

11/16/87 – I have taken this eight-hour-a-day job because it appeals to me on a number of different levels. I love the work and think I will be good at it. But I think it's certainly a disadvantage that I only spend eight hours a day at it. Once I go home other concerns completely take over my life. I think that if I wanted to be completely successful as an apprentice at this point, I would stop teaching Rhetoric, divorce my family, give up plans of finishing my Ph.D., and just eat, sleep, and bind books.

12/30/87 – Six months on the job now. It certainly is much easier now than it was in July. My absences this fall (due to my father's last illness) have made rhythm in my work impossible. I have been here for a month straight now and I am back to enjoying work like I did in July and August. It feels good.

1/26/88 – The teaching that goes on during the day is all of a very informal nature. When I get stuck in my work, I take it to Bill and ask him about it. Or I ask someone else. We learn from each other all day long. We learn more than one approach to solving a problem, and feel like Bill is learning from us too. We have jobs that each performs, as well as the freedom to make models and try things on our own. It is structure without suffocation.

✧ ✧ ✧

When Bill had owned his business in Chicago, the role of his apprentices had been clearly defined: they provided him with assistance in a production setting. They were paid and had to learn techniques quickly to produce and work on the jobs that came into the shop from libraries, businesses, and private clients. Their learning fit what jobs were at hand.

The apprentices that Bill took on in Iowa differed. We did not have to produce work on a schedule to bring in money. Bill no longer had to worry about overhead or buying supplies and could take his time to teach us, work on his historical models, and do conservation work.

However, we still had to meet the same high standards that he had always expected of his apprentices. We were expected to do our work well and in a timely manner. But it was nice not to feel the pressure of producing income—there are enough pressures when you face a valuable book in pieces and need to reassemble it better than it was before.

The first fall I worked for Bill, my father was seriously ill.

I had to fly home several times while he had a number of operations and, finally, for his funeral. Bill never made me feel bad about being gone so much. (This was before the library administration began awarding and keeping track of our sick leave and vacation time as if we were regular employees.) Dedication to family was on a par with dedication to work as far as Bill was concerned. I kept track of my hours of absence and made them up over lunch hours and on weekends. Bill went through the motions of signing our absence slips, but never worried about our hours.

As Bill's apprentices, we worked primarily on conservation treatments of books in the Main Library's Special Collections. We worked on individual items from the collections as David Schoonover, curator of rare books, saw fit to send down to us. Or Bill would purposely choose something off the shelf that needed a type of treatment an apprentice was learning to do. Shortly after Bill had taken his position as university conservator, a plan had been established for which collections of items needed treatment immediately—such as the Leigh Hunt Collection, the History of Hydraulics Collection, the erotica, and the Dada Collection.

The first summer of my apprenticeship we worked on treating and making boxes for items in the Whitman Collection, specifically all of the editions of *Leaves of Grass* since the library had just acquired the last two needed to complete the set. Each box was covered in the same deep green cloth that Bill had chosen specifically—a color I now always think of as Whitman green. Since all the boxes were the same, we got pretty wild with their labels so that they'd have some distinguishing feature. I went to a great deal of trouble to rummage in the decorated paper drawer to find a scrap of marbled paper that suggested "leaves" for stamping the label of the 1872 edition.

Work on the Dada Collection was completed shortly after I started in the department. Most of those works had been printed on very acidic paper akin to newsprint. For their protection, Bill had devised a new style of binding. The Dada works—mostly soft-cover pamphlets—were disbound and washed and deacidified in the usual manner. Then the pages were encapsulated between thin sheets of Mylar using the ultrasonic welder developed by William Minter, one of Bill's former apprentices. The Mylar-clad pages were then gathered together, drilled through a Mylar flap left long on the gutter side, tied, and glued into a strong cloth-covered case binding. Bill's method not only securely protected the fragile text pages so that they could be read, but the books also opened enough to allow the pages to be photocopied by scholars. The first time Bill showed me one of these bindings, he exclaimed, "You could read this book in the bathtub or while you eat spaghetti, and not hurt the pages." He looked at me closely and smiled, "But you won't!"

That summer work on the older pieces of erotica in Special Collections was also completed shortly after I began working in conservation. Some of the books were very explicit. One particular volume, *The Horn Book: A Girl's Guide to the Knowledge of Good and Evil*, printed in London in 1899, was in need of full conservation treatment. It was taken apart and washed and deacidified. While it dried after these treatments, there was quite a bit of traffic past the drying racks. Their shelves were pulled out just enough to allow us to read the pages spread out to dry. Several debates occurred about why words such as "gamahuching" had fallen out of use. Bill seemed relieved when all the erotica was finally returned to Special Collections.

I did get in on the beginning of treating the Szathmary Collection of Culinary Arts, an extensive gathering of books on the culinary arts and sciences that Bill had been instrumental in getting donated to the library. While he was in business in Chicago, Bill had treated Chef Louis's books, stored on the floor above The Bakery, the chef's famous restaurant in Lincoln Park. When Bill learned that Chef Louis was interested in donating the collection to an institution that would care for them properly, he informed the library and university administrators, and they convinced the chef to donate a large portion of his culinary collection to Iowa. We treated and built protective enclosures for the oldest books in this collection as soon as the library received them. Since I had a passion for cooking, I always enjoyed working on the chef's books—especially the eighteenth-century volumes containing illustrations of how to construct towers of French pastries or how to carve every type of fish.

The vaults and rooms that housed the books of Special Collections seemed wondrous to me. Occasionally we were allowed behind the locked doors of the stacks to work on items for exhibit at the tables in the Chef Louis Room or to use the books in the Guild of Book Workers Library that came to be housed in Special Collections in 1987. But for the most part it was off limits. Bill would spend a morning checking over the books we had worked on, taking them up to Special Collections on a library book truck. Much later he would come back down with the cart full of items needing work; we were not privy to what happened in between. But it was like Christmas as he passed out the books that needed treatment. He would take a few books off the truck at a time, bringing some to each of us. It was so exciting to see the new projects we would be working on.

Bill would arrive just behind me, waiting for me to move to one side so that he could place the books on my bench. He would show each one to me briefly, roughly detailing the type of conservation treatment each one would need. When I was first working on learning leather rebacking, Bill gave me a three-volume set of Sir Walter Scott's writings from 1810. I knew I had learned leather rebacking pretty well when six months later he brought me a partial leather rebacking to do on an incunabulum printed in 1477. When he was planning a workshop on pamphlet binding, Bill brought me a series of pamphlets from the John P. Vander Maas Collection of Railroadiana. I completed a whole series of treatments on them so that he would have examples to show the workshop participants.

One of the side effects of Bill's death was that first Larry, as senior apprentice, and then gradually the rest of us, were allowed increased access to the stacks in Special Collections. I was allowed to roam up and down the aisles looking for books that interested me to work on or that pertained to a style or aspect of binding I was studying. It was a fabulous privilege—one I never took for granted—and the one thing I hated most to lose when my apprenticeship ended.

But apprentices also had more mundane jobs to perform. We were expected to keep the back work counter and sink clean. When they got dirty and no one took the initiative to clean up, Bill would point it out. He liked everything neat. We were also expected to keep our benches in order. Bill's was almost always tidy—even when he was in the middle of a complicated treatment. He didn't wear a work apron except when using leather dye. "If you wear an apron, you expect to make a mess," he would say. "If you don't wear an apron, you will force yourself to be neater." Surprisingly, this held true for me except in cases of extreme clumsiness.

We were also expected to give demonstrations for various tours that came through the department. Bill would ask each of us what we were working on before the tour group arrived and have one person washing a book, something spread out in the drying racks, someone sewing, and so on to illustrate the steps of a full conservation treatment. He would show the group around the department and exhibit the models and finished examples of work. As he brought people to each work area, we were expected to explain what we were doing and answer any questions from the group.

The first time I had to do this, I was terrified. It was the afternoon that the Friends of the Library came through the department in four small groups in conjunction with their annual dinner. We had spent most of the day before cleaning up the back counter and the benches and putting out books and models for viewing. Larry washed a book, I sewed, and other student workers mended pages and constructed cases. But the book I had chosen to sew was comprised of only eight sections of pages. By the time the first tour group finished in the department, I had sewn it completely. So in the few minutes before the second group came through, I cut it apart again. By the time the afternoon was over, I had sewn the same book four times.

○ ○ ○

2/16/88 — A lot of discussion during the last week has been given over to defining a "fine" binding. It seems from what I've heard that the materials and craftsmanship for a fine binding need to be the best. Great care must be taken to get everything exact, perfect. You use what papers and glues you need to achieve the affect you want and don't worry about their effects on the life of the book.

Preferably you design a binding that is compatible with the interior design of the book.

But there are also conservators who do fine bindings with archival papers and safer adhesives who say that fine bindings shouldn't hurt a text block. I've seen fine leather bindings put on books in such a way that to open the book to read them would break the cover. It seems pointless to me to put a cover on a book that isn't reader friendly. That makes them art objects. But maybe I feel this way because I was a reader of books long before I became a binder.

4/4/88 — I just finished rebacking three volumes of Sir Walter Scott. Yuck! I really mauled them! The leather spines I pared and dyed were only just wide enough and I had trouble getting them to fit.

My problem is that I hate doing more than one of the same thing. Since I am not good at rebacking, I did it poorly three times over and I find that difficult. It is very frustrating to be bad at something. Of course, I know that the only way to get better is to reback over and over again. But I feel stuck in limbo, mauling books. I guess in a way that's what being an apprentice is all about: being bad repeatedly until you get good. Or at least better.

◌ ◌ ◌

It was difficult to be an apprentice in a system that tried to make us into university employees without all their benefits. Under the terms of my NEA grant, I received health and dental insurance. Bill had told me my salary for the first year and assured that each year after that I would receive a raise of $1,000, but actually, my salary was controlled by the library administration, and at the beginning of my second year I received a raise of $112.50 for the entire year. Just fifty cents more than my parking sticker cost me.

It also wasn't assured that my grant would *be* renewed each year, which was why I was cautious at first not to give up teaching rhetoric at night and why I didn't immediately drop out of graduate school. I was afraid that my apprenticeship, like a dream, would come quickly to an end after one year, and I would be left with nothing to do, no way to support myself. Bill did not have the power to promise me that I would absolutely be employed for a five- to seven-year term, even though he acted like I certainly would be.

But he was in charge of my training and had complete freedom to define my duties and assign the books I would treat. Bill obviously had the experience and confidence to take on apprentices—I was number six in the chain. But that by no means meant that he was always a perfect craftsman. He too occasionally made mistakes while treating an object or while tooling a leather cover—the latter always a risky operation.

The first time I realized that Bill could make a mistake, it was quite a shock. I had been so absorbed in my own ability to make mistakes that it had never occurred to me that Bill could do something wrong. I had just completed a sketchbook that I planned to use for mapping out my garden and keeping track of each spring's plantings. It had a maroon leather spine that extended over onto the front and back covers a bit, the rest covered with marbled paper (not a practical design for a book I intended to drag into the garden with me, although I didn't realize it at the time). When it was completed, Bill suggested that I tool a blind line down the edges of the leather that butted up against the marbled paper for a decorative effect. I agreed. In the beginning, I always agreed with his suggestions.

Bill showed me how to mark where the line would go with my dividers, evenly spacing it just along the edges of the marbled paper on both covers. He showed me how to put the impression on the leather with the tip of my bone folder. "I'll show you how to put the line on the back cover and you can do the front," he instructed. He plugged in the hotplate used for heating up tools and warmed up a piece of line, a small brass strip set into a wooden handle. Bill tested to see that it was the right temperature by touching it against a piece of natural sponge wet in a bowl and listening to the hiss. Then he began to run the hot tool up the impression in the leather. Two-thirds of the way up, the tool jumped its groove and in a heartbeat had made a parallel line for the rest of the impression. Railroad tracks. I stood there staring. Not only had Bill made a mistake, he had messed up the cover of *my* book.

Noticing the look on my face, Bill said, "The mark of a good craftsman is his ability to correct his mistakes." Bill explained that the double line could be eased back out of the leather, but that it would probably be simpler just to make the entire line double, front and back. I agreed. Bill heated up another piece of line that made a double rule and repeated the procedure on the front cover. When he finished, I couldn't tell that it hadn't meant to be that way. I repeated the procedure on the back cover, although with the newness of the experience and my natural fear of handling the hot tool, my double lines turned out slightly wavy in places. Bill's were perfectly straight.

Bill never made me feel inept for having done something incorrectly, though he occasionally teased me about it if he felt I was taking myself too seriously. He suggested ways the mistake could be corrected and helped me examine why it had happened in the first place. In final evaluations of my books, he first praised what had gone well and then discussed the problems. It was a manner of teaching that I tried to adopt when I later had my own binding students. It helped me not to be afraid to try something new. And it always helped to keep a sense of humor.

IN THE
PUBLIC EYE

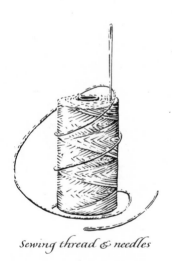

Sewing thread & needles

TALENT SEARCH TO DEFRAY
REFURBISHING IOWA'S CONSTITUTION

Iowa is facing a constitutional crisis.

Secretary of State Elaine Baxter personally chauf-
feured the 130-year-old constitution to Iowa City last
March so that the deteriorating document could be
restored.

The restoration, which was supposed to take two
months, still is not done because of the resignation of
the only person in the state government with the
expertise to preserve the priceless document.

The state has not been able to hire another paper
conservator to perform the delicate restoration, so the
40-page, leather-bound document has been returned
to Baxter's office in the Statehouse, where its brittle
pages continue to yellow and molder.

—*Des Moines Register*, November 27, 1987

It all began on the afternoon of April 29, 1988, when Secretary
of State Elaine Baxter drove the Iowa State constitution from
her office in Des Moines to the university's Main Library in
Iowa City. Accompanied by police escort, Baxter had driven
carefully with the volume held by Deputy Secretary of State
Paulee Lipsman. Bill, in his good navy suit, was waiting on

the steps of the library when Baxter arrived. The constitution, secured in bubble wrap and brown paper for its ride, was carried into the library and presented to Bill and University Librarian Sheila Creth by Baxter in the middle of a small media circus. Footage on the news programs that evening showed Bill looking serious as he examined the document in the immaculate Conservation Department. Behind the circle of reporters, I caught occasional glimpses of the apprentices and student workers.

That had been our place all day. We had cleaned the lab and cleared a bench so that Bill would have a place to examine the constitution for the media. He stood at the bench with Baxter and Creth, the photographers in front taking pictures, and us in the background not really saying or doing anything. Bill held the book facing the cameras and paged through it. He picked it up and talked to Baxter and Creth about it. We were just fixtures in the department. I was fascinated to see how such a simple thing as handing over a book to someone could become such a public event. It was a far cry from Bill bringing books down from Special Collections on a cart.

The constitution had been a relatively unnoticed document residing in the secretary of state's office in Des Moines, where it was locked in a glass-topped wooden case atop a pedestal that looked like a lectern. The constitution was open to the first page, held securely with clear plastic clips attached with screws. A photocopy of the last page of the constitution, bearing the signatures of its signers, rested on the blank page across from the title page. The case was in a corner of the office next to an air conditioner.

When Baxter became secretary of state in January 1987, she also became keeper of the constitution. Noticing that it wasn't in the best of shape, she began looking into having it restored. This April trip wasn't the first time she had brought the book to Iowa City.

Baxter's efforts to have the constitution restored had begun in March 1987, when she first drove the document to Iowa City. Sharlane Grant, conservator of the State Historical Society, was to perform the restoration. Grant had evaluated the volume at the state capitol in February and recommended treatment: the volume was to be disbound, the pages dry-cleaned, washed, deacidified, and then encapsulated in protective Mylar. The original leather cover would be restored and bound around a facsimile of the document for display purposes. But when Grant left Iowa to take another job, the treatment was never performed.

The next fall, Jane Meggers, the conservator who succeeded Grant at the Historical Society, began taking Bill's night class and working with us at the library three aftenoons a week on advanced conservation treatments. She was approached by her superiors about restoring the state constitution according to Grant's plan. But Jane felt that it was silly for her to do the treatment when one of the best-known book conservators in the country was working in the university's Main Library, just across town. She approached Bill informally about restoring the constitution, and when he agreed that he'd consider doing the job, Jane convinced the Historical Society to recommend him to the secretary of state.

Negotiations to restore the constitution had begun after a newspaper article detailing the state's dilemma prompted letters and calls from across the state and country—many mentioning that there was, in fact, a wonderful conservator in Iowa City, Bill Anthony. Baxter got in touch with the library and invited Bill to inspect the document in her office, which he did on December 8, 1987. He took two pages of notes with diagrams detailing the construction and condition of the volume. After some consideration, he wrote up a proposal for treating the constitution and sent it to the secretary of state early in January 1988.

Once when I sought Bill's advice about how to prepare an estimate for a private client, he told me I should take a good look at the work to be done, estimate the cost of the materials and labor, and then double that amount for my final quote. "Things are always more complicated than you think at first," he told me, "and they always take longer to do than you thought they would." In his rough draft of the treatment proposal for the state constitution sent to the university library's administrative assistant to be typed, Bill cited an estimate for the conservation job at $5,000. In the final version sent to Secretary of State Baxter, this amount was $10,000, not including the cost of "a new case built to house the volume safely," to be built at the university.

Bill's treatment plan varied from the one originally proposed by Grant at the State Historical Society. He proposed to disbind the document, dry-clean, wash, and deacidify the pages, repair their tears with Japanese mending tissue made by Tim Barrett at the University of Iowa Papermaking Facility, resew the volume, and finally put it back in its original calf-leather binding. Bill would also make a facsimile with a similar binding that could be used for display purposes outside of the statehouse. Protective drop-spine boxes were to be made to house both volumes during transportation and for storage of the facsimile. Baxter approved the treatment proposal and brought the constitution back to Iowa City.

○   ○   ○

In my own work, I continued backward through the history of bookbinding in my conservation treatments. That spring I moved through the nineteenth century with its weak leather bindings into the late eighteenth century, whose books weren't much better. In one of his book distributions that March, Bill piled on my desk several two- and three-volume sets to work on. Two volumes of *Gay's Fables* from the 1730s. Two volumes of *Specimens of the Table Talk of the Late Samuel Taylor Coleridge*, published in the 1830s. And from the first decade of the nineteenth century, there was Sir Walter Scott. Volumes and volumes of Sir Walter Scott. I received several different sets that included varying combinations of *Lady of* the Lake, *The Lay of the Last Minstrel, Marmion,* and *Lord of the Isles.* All had covers of tooled brown calf. All had covers moments away from falling off or already past that point. The loner was a book titled *A Complete Course of Lithography.* I fell in love with it instantly because its leather was maroon, it had a three-quarter marbled paper cover, and there was only *one* of it.

Bill set these volumes in piles along the top of my bench while I watched in dismay. There were definitely times when I didn't care for his practice of giving us a lot of the same types of treatments to do at the same time. I understood the principle behind it: we'd get better at a task if we repeated it over and over again. That was one of the principles of apprenticeship. He said very nicely, "This will give you some practice with leather rebacking." I already had judged these books by their covers and didn't like what I saw.

When manuscript books were first covered in leather over wooden boards before the sixteenth century, binders used heavy skins of full thickness. This supported the weight of the heavy boards and thick text blocks where the books opened at the flex point of the hinge on the covers. The skins and the books held up well.

But once the invention of printing in the late fifteenth century dramatically speeded up the production of books, bookbinding styles had to change. As text blocks became smaller and thinner and covers came to be made of cardboard, the leathers that covered them thinned down as well.

By the eighteenth and nineteenth centuries the leathers were pared thin so that they were easier to handle and looked more elegant on the books. But such treatment of the skins caused them to break down much more quickly—especially in the hinge area that receives the most stress as the book is opened and closed. The volumes Bill had given me to work on were fine examples of that breaking-down process. Learning to reback a book in leather was the mainstay of many book conservators' jobs. Many people have family Bibles they want restored, and almost all of these Bibles have thick heavy text blocks bound in thin leather with covers that have broken free.

○ ○ ○

Anthony to restore Iowa constitution at UI laboratory

Iowa's 131-year-old state constitution will be saved from the wear and tear of time so it can be passed on through future generations thanks to the efforts of UI libraries book conservator William Anthony. . . .

"I feel very honored that they asked me to conserve such an important document," Anthony said.

UI Libraries Director Sheila Creth said she was pleased Anthony's expertise and experience was being recognized by state officials. . . . The conservation project, which will cost the state $10,000, will take approximately 6 to 8 weeks. Anthony and his two apprentices will remove the document's binding, remove machine stitching on the pages, and then dry clean the pages before washing and deacidifying them with magnesium bicarbonate. . . .

> Anthony said although the document is very important, it will not be difficult to restore.
>
> "There are no risks for a person who is qualified," he said. "It's a very simple document—it's hand-written on 40 pages of good quality handmade paper, but it's quite dirty and has been exposed to not very clean air for a long time."
>
> ... While it is at the UI for preservation, the document will be stored in a vault in Main Library.
>
> —*Daily Iowan*, April 29, 1988

Once the media attention from the constitution's arrival had died down, life in the department seemed to get back to normal. We had come to ignore the jokes being made about how Bill was "reconstituting" the constitution. But because of this document's importance, reporters and photographers periodically intruded into our quiet space. The University Libraries were themselves making a slide documentary on the conservation process to be loaned out to interested people and schoolchildren all over Iowa. Other photographers and television reporters showed up occasionally to record the progress being made. Bill did the restoration of the constitution himself. But the rest of us were given related tasks to do as well.

Jane got the job of photocopying the manuscript pages of the constitution for the facsimile that would be used for public display outside of the state capitol building. Although Bill could use sophisticated machinery like the ultrasonic welder for encapsulating book pages, he never used a copier for more than the most mundane of chores.

Bound, the original constitution was just a little over eleven by seventeen inches. Since the facsimile was to be made on acid-free paper, Jane cut down some of the stock we kept in the department closest in color to the cream of the original so it would fit into the eleven-by-seventeen-inch tray of a copy machine. Test runs made on the library administration's aging photocopier showed that Jane would have to find a newer machine to use for this job. She wrapped the original constitution and the paper prepared for the facsimile in brown kraft paper, placed them into her khaki-colored shoulder bag, and pedaled uphill from the library to a copier store in town, a slightly less formal trip for the volume than its journey from Des Moines.

The text of the constitution was written in copperplate, a cursive business script of the eighteenth century often used for public documents like the Declaration of Independence. The manuscript was legible, even though the first page of the text and the facing blank page were slightly soiled from being handled and from having been exposed while the book was on display. The text was written in iron gall ink that had turned brown with age. The signature page of the constitution—the final and most interesting page—was the dirtiest of all.

Jane's first efforts at photocopying the document failed. As we examined the copy, we could see there were places where the spidery writing wasn't dark enough to read, even though she had experimented with the darkness level on the copier. After three attempts, Jane eventually made a successful facsimile of the pages using the copy machine at the State Historical Society. Not one to waste things—especially a large quantity of acid-free paper—Jane cut down the failed facsimiles and test runs and made notepads out of them. For almost a year we wrote notes and took phone messages in the Conservation Department on the back of spidery fragments of the state constitution.

○ ○ ○

I was approached late that summer by one of the directors of the University of Iowa's Arts Outreach Program to teach for them. Through this program, graduate students and faculty members at the university prepare a class they can teach to schoolchildren of various ages and abilities. A brochure is sent out in the fall, and schools schedule the artists they want to come and visit during the next school year. The artists are paid for their preparation and receive an hourly fee to teach their class. After I was interviewed and accepted, Bill gave his approval, and I signed up to teach no more than two days a month.

Bill was very supportive: "This will be a good experience for you." The Conservation Department provided supplies, and I worked out a series of simple bindings at home that I could teach in a thirty- to fifty-minute class period in an elementary school. I went to a local art supply store and found potter's tools that would pass for folders and awls. I had it all planned: I would arrive in a classroom filled with fresh, eager young faces, pull out my red-and-yellow plastic pencil boxes of tools and my stacks of paper, neatly cut on the board shear, and teach docile schoolchildren all over Iowa the joys of bookbinding.

My first workshop at Brown School in Davenport was a real eye-opener. I was sent to a classroom where there was a videotape recorder set up. Not only were they paying me to come, they were going to tape my session to play for other classes. I performed for a group of fourth graders, finally allowed into the room after being admonished to avoid the wires and video tripod. The children kept up with my demonstrations, making books of their own as the camera followed me around the room. I was relieved when it was over.

I packed up my supplies and moved to another classroom, where I repeated my performance for a class of fifth graders. Then I did it again for another class of fourth graders. Next I was rushed off to be treated to lunch in the school cafeteria. After one look, I stayed away from the hot dogs, cooked carrots, and Tater Tots with cheese sauce and opted for a chef's salad—short on the chef, long on the salad.

My last session of the day was with a group of parent volunteers who worked in the school library's writing center. Children told their stories to the volunteers, who typed them into a computer and printed them out. Then the volunteers helped the students pick out cover paper from voluminous wallpaper sample books and stapled them together. I was proudly shown a whole table full of these books covered with flocked bathroom wallpapers and sophisticated foil-striped hallway wallpapers and chipper teapot kitchen wallpapers. Other students in the school checked out these books to read. The volunteers wanted my suggestions for more durable binding styles. They had resorted to stapling the texts into the wallpaper covers since they were no longer allowed to use rubber cement with its dangerous fumes.

I was put on the spot. In the Conservation Department I had access to some of the most expensive papers from England and the United States to use as I pleased. It had been years since I had been made heady by the smell of rubber cement. I needed to recommend something they could use easily with children. I suggested they could use glue sticks and double-sided tape, or sew the books together. Pleased with the idea, they looked at my sample pamphlet binding, and I demonstrated it for them.

I took four sheets of the computer paper used for the children's stories and folded them once down the middle the short way. Glancing quickly through the wallpaper sample book, I picked out a sheet with green and white stripes with wooden spoons and folded it around the computer paper. Then I poked three holes through the fold: one in the middle, and two close to the outer edges. Taking up a needle threaded with a piece of black yarn, I began to sew, detailing the shape of a capital B. From the outside to the inside through the center hole. Back out the bottom hole. Up to the top hole and back inside. Out again through the middle. Tie off. The volunteers decided it looked easy and fell to making their own samples covered with rose-covered bedroom wallpaper.

"How did it go?" Bill asked the next morning when I went back to work.

"Fine," I answered. I still hadn't quite gotten over the sensation of being wrung out like a washcloth so that the school got its fifty-four dollars' worth out of me. "It wasn't quite what I expected." Bill didn't question me any further.

A week later I was in the basement of someone's home at a local Montessori preschool. Two frazzle-haired teachers helped me demonstrate the same big-B pamphlet binding to preschoolers using giant, dull-pointed crewel needles. Once we had prepared the folded pages for the children to sew, I asked about covers. One of the teachers went over to a cupboard and dragged out several wallpaper sample books with swatches hanging loose as if they'd been shuffled badly. I was glad I had a month off before my next workshop in Vinton.

○ ○ ○

Bill began giving me work from private clients to do. People would call or drop by the department with items that needed repair. Older people who came to the University Hospitals for treatments or doctor visits would make their way across campus to see him with family treasures tucked under their arms. Bill did very few of these himself, doling them out to

Larry to work on privately. We were allowed to do work for private clients in the department before or after hours, over lunch, or on weekends. We were expected to reimburse the library for any supplies we used.

Bill approached my bench one day carrying a volume of Mark Twain that belonged to one of the library administrators. It was a nineteenth-century cloth binding and had some water damage to the front cover. "She wants the cover cleaned up a bit," Bill explained. "Just wipe over the stains with a bit of colored methyl cellulose. Then write out a bill for what you want to charge." Bill put the book down on my bench and walked away.

I was aghast. Here this person had brought this book to the department to be "cleaned up," expecting Bill's expert touch. It was someone I saw in the library break room every day. What if I made the cover worse? I was tempted to give it back to Bill, but I knew very well that he wouldn't have given it to me to take care of if I weren't capable of fixing it. And I had no idea what to charge.

That day over my lunch hour, I mixed up a bit of methyl cellulose, adding little dabs of green and gray acrylic until a sample painted on a piece of scrap paper and dried approximated the dark green cloth on the book. Then I took one of the large cotton "orifice swabs" a student worker in the department brought us from the hospital and coated it lightly with the colored methyl cellulose. Carefully, I dabbed at the water-faded spots of the cover. The color covered the water spots, but when they dried they looked mottled. The cover looked worse. A large pit opened in my stomach. I was starting to panic. I didn't know what to do next.

I put the book aside for a few minutes, forcing myself to go into the break room and eat my lunch. Then I came back and examined the book. The new color was correct, but the rough texture produced by my application of the methyl cellulose and acrylic didn't match the smooth surface of the rest of the cover.

I took a large piece of cotton and dabbed it into some more of the green color and gently smoothed it over the entire surface of the cover just once, as quickly and evenly as I possibly could. I knew from other forays with nineteenth-century cloth covers that if I lingered too long or stroked too hard, the colored surface of the book cloth would get too moist and start to come off all over. I let the cover dry and examined it again. It looked much smoother than it had before. After lunch I took it up to Bill.

"This looks good," Bill said. "How much do you want for the repair?"

I'd sweated over this part, too. "Ten dollars?"

"That seems fair," he replied. It wasn't possible for anyone to reimburse me enough for panic. Bill later took the book off and came back with a check for me—my first pay from a private job. I was in no hurry to do another one.

I began to pay more attention to the people who came in with items to be repaired. They seemed to fall into two categories.

The first consisted of professional people who needed something fixed because it was falling apart—something they used often in their lines of work. One of my early clients was a lawyer in West Branch, Iowa. He had county maps he used often bound into a large, unwieldy volume. As a result of constant use, they were tearing out of the book. He had mended them with clear tape, and it was also coming off. He wanted the five maps he used most often taken out of the book and put into a more usable form. I pulled them from the volumes, removed the tape, mended and spray-deacidified them, and encapsulated them in Mylar. Now they were flat and easily accessible, the way he needed them to be.

The second type who brought things into our department had a family treasure they wanted to keep to pass on to a child or grandchild—usually a family Bible. But Bibles were tricky. Typically large and unwieldy, they were often made with inexpensive materials and leather. Often the text block had broken down into chunks along the length of the spine from the weight of the book straining the binding when it was opened.

Some clients with family treasures seemed willing to pay whatever it cost to repair the treasure, others only the barest minimum. They would often ask Bill, "Do you think this is worth having fixed?" Over and over I would hear him say, "If this book has value to you, then it is worth having fixed."

He talked to me once about Bibles after a client had been in. She wanted her father's Bible restored to its full glory, but wasn't willing to pay for it. Bill finally satisfied her with an alternate solution. The woman left the book to be restored and Bill showed it to me. "She wants the book put back as good as new," he said, "but the text block is about to break into so many pieces that just resewing it would cost several hundred dollars." He gently opened the Bible to the middle where it separated cleanly into two halves.

"These are the pages that matter." He held the book gently, and I saw we were looking at the pages dividing the Old Testament from the New. "These are the pages of family history," he continued. "Who married whom when. The list of their children and their baptisms and marriages. These are the pages that make this Bible valuable."

"What are you going to do?" I asked.

"Well, she was interested in having it all put back together the way it was before. When I told her how much it would cost, she didn't want to pay that. So I am going to remove these pages, wash, deacidify, and encapsulate them. Then I will make her a box to house the pieces of the Bible and these sheets." He looked at me. "If she wants to read the Bible, she can always get another copy. These are the pages that her father read and that will matter to her children."

○ ○ ○

My next excursion into the world of teaching bookbinding was with two other Arts Outreach teachers: David, a graduate student in music, and Rachel, a graduate student in drama.

We had been hired by a rural school to spend the day with three grade levels of their talented and gifted students. We chatted all the way down the interstate about how well our classes would go. The music student had brought a trunk full of percussion instruments with him; the drama student dragged a duffel bag of scarves and hats. I had my cardboard box of tools and neat stacks of paper, this time including construction paper for the covers.

We arrived at the school to discover that we would be working with the students in the church hall next door, each of us assigned a room to work in. Rachel got the auditorium, David and I got smaller classrooms. The students would rotate among the three of us: one group before lunch, two after. We set up in our respective rooms and waited. The students were having a morning snack in the large, open lobby—homemade cookies and pop their mothers had provided for this special occasion. By the time we got them, they were wired and ready to run.

I had decided after my first workshop that I needed to place bookbinding in context for my students. I had brought along several historical models to talk about the days when books were covered with wooden boards and leather. But the students couldn't sit still to listen: too much sugar running through their blood. When one little boy in the back stood up on his chair, I quickly passed out the paper supplies. Another little boy flew the first paper airplane, crafted out of a lovely shade of blue construction paper, across the room as I passed out the needles and thread I had brought. It got worse from there.

"Don't throw the folders!" I found myself screaming.

"Sit down!"

"Pay attention!"

Fifty minutes later, four students had finished their bindings. The others left the room with a collection of paper scraps and some yarn. Back in the lobby, their mothers had pizza and more pop for lunch with brownies for dessert.

Rachel, David, and I ate ours in one corner of the room. All of us had had the same awful experience of being unable to control our students. Rachel suggested strangulation with scarves. David thought about bashing heads between cymbals. I contemplated sewing mouths together with yarn. The day didn't improve.

We rode home discussing how they'd paid us to teach, but we'd been glorified baby-sitters. Few of the students had learned anything. We wondered if all talented and gifted students were so "energetic" or if it was just their diet. I had another month to recover.

The next workshop I taught was an evening class at a progressive boarding school in the country. The students were high schoolers, much older than I had taught so far, and I prepared an accordion book design that their art teacher said they could use in their landscape drawing class. I taught in a lovely, large art room with nice long tables. So far I had been teaching in regular classrooms with the students confined to school desks or small tables. Here the students had room to spread out.

They had even more room to spread out because only eight of them showed up. My class was an "evening optional activity." I could tell I bored them. At least, I bored seven of them. They could have been at some other evening activity but had chosen me and I bored them. Only one young man seemed interested. He was tall and lanky with a mop of blond hair that fell continually into his eyes. While listening to my explanations of the samples I brought and watching my demonstration, he leaned back in his chair, his long fingers moving a pencil that filled his blank pages with landscapes of rolling cornfields, barns, and fields with horses—the scenery that surrounded the school. He had sketched so quickly that when he finished his binding, it was complete inside and out.

When I had completed my demonstration, the others got up and left, but he stayed to help me put things away and pack up my supplies. The teacher who escorted me to the room never came back, so the young man walked me to my car, carrying my box of supplies. He chatted on excitedly about how he could use this book design for an art project he was working on.

As I drove home, I was happy that I had helped one person see something new about books. But I couldn't shake the sensation of those other fourteen bored eyes staring at me all evening, suffering as if I were penance they were forced to do. I was beginning to have third and fourth thoughts about teaching bookbinding, about going forth to teach school-children all over Iowa. Winter break saved me from another workshop for two months.

The next time I was on the road again in a university car heading down the interstate, I was joined once again by Rachel. We were off to a school in West Des Moines to teach a whole day's worth of workshops. We left Iowa City very early in the morning and stopped at a truck stop for coffee and doughnuts, worried about how the day would go. We got lost and arrived at the school with only a few minutes to spare. As soon as we entered the building, a teacher met us and whisked us off to our separate rooms where students were eagerly awaiting us.

I was up on the second floor of this older building. The students I was to start with had been sitting patiently waiting for me as their teacher read to them. I set up quickly and began. For forty-five minutes they folded paper and watched my demonstrations, and sewed and talked. They never got out of their chairs or threw the supplies. They raised their hands when they had questions. I was amazed by this nice group of third graders.

When the bell rang I was whisked downstairs to a sunny room full of second graders. There was barely enough room to move between the desks, but they waited patiently as I showed my samples, gave my demonstrations, and moved to help those who couldn't thread their needles with the yarn we were sewing with. This had amazed me the first few times I had done these workshops, that there were children—mostly boys—who didn't know how to thread a needle. In this class there was a young man who quickly threaded his needle and then helped those around him to thread theirs. When I complimented him on his talent, he replied, "My granny taught me how. I sew with her." I was charmed.

Two hours later, Rachel and I were reunited in the teachers' lounge for lunch.

"We didn't think you'd want to eat in the cafeteria," one of the teachers said to me. "So we all brought things for a salad lunch." There were two long tables covered with bowls. Midwest Jell-O salads. Seven-layer salads. Lettuce salads. Pasta salads. I had never seen so many salads. There were breads and drinks as well. Rachel and I sat and ate and chatted our way through two periods of lunch with the teachers who cycled through. "This is a treat for us, too," one exclaimed.

I complimented one of the teachers whose students I'd worked with on how well behaved they had been. "Thank you," she replied. "The students have been so excited about your coming. When we got the brochure about the Arts Outreach teachers last fall, the students voted on the two they most wanted to come. Then they had bake sales and other fund-raising activities for months to raise the fees for the workshops. We have nothing in our budget for extras like this." She finished her diet pop and went back out the door. Rachel and I did two more workshops before we drove home, exhausted and amazed at how well the day had gone.

I did three more workshops before the semester ended. I faced more energetic talented and gifted students and more bored high schoolers. But the trip to West Des Moines had made the whole string of ordeals worth it.

I told Bill at the end of May that the Arts Outreach coordinator had called and asked me if I wanted to be in the program again the next year. I told him I'd declined. "It was a lot of work," he said. I agreed. I told him I didn't think that bookbinding for schoolchildren was the kind I wanted to teach. Two weeks later he came up behind me at the corner of my bench and asked me if I'd like to design a class to teach—an intermediate class to go between Larry's and his in the Saturday and Evening Program. He wanted students to have more experience with adhesive bindings before they took on special projects with him. I said yes immediately. My experience as a journeyman was over.

○ ○ ○

Off and on throughout that spring and summer, journalists got in touch with the library, wanting to do interviews with Bill while he was working on the constitution. He never actually said anything about it, but I think these visits were a nuisance to him. The restoration of the state constitution was a straightforward treatment—nothing as complicated as what he had done to conserve Northwestern University's elephant folios of Audubon's *Birds of America,* a treatment he was extremely proud of. Once he showed me photographs of himself holding up one of the enormous volumes after treatment.

He was young enough so that his hair was red rather than gray. I think he was also proud to be doing the constitution, but a little tired, for some reason, of the limelight.

Bill taped one interview that summer to coincide with the washing of the text after the volume had been disbound and the pages dry-cleaned. Watching the pages of a book—especially a manuscript like this one—be submerged in a tray of water never failed to amaze people. Bright white lights were set up around the washing sink and the interviewer asked questions as Bill, dressed as always in nice pants, oxford shirt with the sleeves rolled up, and no apron, floated the pages into the distilled water. We worked at our benches, keeping as quiet as possible while the taping was going on.

While the fuss over the pages of the constitution continued and Bill was busy doing all the mending, I decided that it was time for me to approach the volumes of Walter Scott majestically gracing one corner of my workbench. As I examined them and took notes on their condition, I saw how many of their covers were off as a result of the thinness and poor condition of the leather in the hinge areas of the bindings. With my lifting knife, Bill had me cut free the covers that barely remained attached.

The volumes were all tight backed. That means the leather that goes over the back of the spine of the book with the pretty raised bands, decorative tooling, and gold titling was glued directly to the back of the sections after they had been glued and lined with an open-weave piece of cloth called "mull." The other way to attach the leather to a book like this is to place it over a hollow paper tube shaped over the spine of the book—a hollow that allows the spine covering of the book to pop back as the book is opened, creating a crescent tube opening along the spine of the book. Books with hollows are very easy to disbind for conservation treatments: you just slit along the edges of the hollow's paper and the spine leather comes off in one beautifully intact piece. That obviously had not been the preferred method of binding Walter Scott.

I attacked one of the sets, beginning with *Lady of the Lake*. I placed scrap book board cut to the same size as the text block on each side, slid the book into the jaws of the backing press, and clamped it securely. Then I began at the top side of the spine leather, trying with my lifting knife to gently raise up the leather spine, away from the mull. I gently pushed my knife under the leather and carefully began to slide it down to try to remove the spine in one piece. A large flake of the spine leather came up and off of the spine on the blade of my knife, taking a chunk out of the decorative element tooled into the top panel of the spine. My heart skipped a beat. I fetched Bill before I did any more damage.

He surveyed my minimal progress and said, "Keep trying. Sometimes once you get it started, it will come off easier and in one strip." Several large leather flakes later, I fetched him again.

He looked carefully at the spine that now looked as if a beaver had been lunching on the top panels of the leather.

The edges were missing, collected carefully in a small glass bowl resting on the side of the backing press. Bill took my lifting knife and began to raise the leather away from the spine. He held the blade at just the right angle so that it flexed deftly under the leather. Sliding it underneath the top two panels, he lost only the tiniest of flakes along the edges.

"Red rot," he commented. This is a condition of aging leather that causes it to break down—usually a result of all the chemicals used to tan and color it. Red rot is the powdery residue that you get all over your hands when you pick up an older leather volume.

"You'll have to go carefully," he continued, handing the lifting knife back to me. "Keep the pieces in their proper order and you can reassemble them on the leather rebacking." My stomach was knotting up even more. Reassemble? That didn't sound like what I should be striving for.

I finally got the leather off the spine in about ten pieces. The two panels Bill had eased up had broken apart at the fake raised spine bands. Now used as decorative elements, the raised leather bands across the backs of leather books had once covered the leather cords that the volume had been sewn on. But with the modernization and "improvement" of binding in the nineteenth century, books were more quickly sewn on flat tapes and the raised spine bands were commonly formed over strips of cardboard. I was dismayed at the mess I had made. Putting the spine back onto the new leather of the rebacking would be like trying to work a decomposing jigsaw puzzle.

"Try another one," Bill said. "This time try covering the spine leather with a piece of kozo first."

For this I brushed the spine of the book with a thin paste and tamped a strip of kozo directly into the leather with a dry brush. Once it had dried, the principle was that it held delicate leather together securely so that it could be lifted up in one piece. Then I could glue the leather spine back down after I rebacked the book, gently removing the kozo by reactivating the paste with a wet cotton swab.

I tried it.

I ended up with a piece of kozo decorated with large chunks of leather. At least I would not have any trouble figuring out how to repiece them. I tried the same technique on the third volume of Scott with not much success. With the spines resting in labeled envelopes, I moved on to rebacking the volumes with new leather. Bill moved from mending to rejoining the single pages of the constitution into conjugate pairs that would then be folded into sections of pages. Photographers kept setting up lights and taking his picture.

⊙ ⊙ ⊙

Ideally, attaching the leather for a rebacking involves gently lifting the leather on the spine edge of the boards extending about half an inch onto the covers and working from the edge closest to the spine. New leather, dyed to approximate the original color, is pared thinly along the edges and slipped under the old leather of the covers. This creates a new bridge of leather from the front cover across the spine of the book to the back cover. The text block is glued out all along the spine and attached to the inside of the new spine leather. Cloth hinges that have been attached to the text block are inserted and glued underneath the paper pastedowns on the insides of the boards, securing the text block inside the cover. Then the original spine piece, ideally intact from head to foot, is glued onto the back of the spine, and the volume now shows new leather only in the hinge areas of the front and back covers. The book has been repaired, approximating as closely as possible its original structure.

When I finished, I ended up with three volumes of Walter Scott that had nicely dyed new leather slipped under the leather of the front and back covers. Unfortunately, the original leather on the covers showed a few crease marks from having been lifted up. The original spines of the volumes had been repieced onto the backs of the volumes—mostly in alignment. Once I had anchored the pieces, Bill had had me paint the spines with a solution of Klucel-G, a synthetic water-soluble adhesive, to try and consolidate the leather so that it would stay intact. Unfortunately, it also made the leather shiny and highlighted the cracks between the pieces. As I wrote up my treatment card for the finished set, I sincerely hoped that no library patron would ever ask to see these volumes from Special Collections.

That was a problem of learning conservation treatments

on actual items from the library's collection. When my inexperience showed, it was on a book that mattered. Although I realized that there were many other editions of Walter Scott in the world, and even in our university libraries, I wanted to do my best on these books from Special Collections. My best as an apprentice wasn't always up to standard. That explained why I hadn't worked backward yet to do treatments on any incunabula from the first fifty years of printing. Of course, they were also printed on better paper and covered with better leather than books I was treating from the seventeenth and eighteenth centuries, and were quite often in better condition.

I liked it much better when Bill gave me single volumes or sets of volumes that had lost one or more covers. Then he usually had me make notes of the exact titling of the spine, type style, and placement of any decorative elements, and just redo the whole cover. I was free to design a new binding, following a pattern suitable for the age of the book. I loved the freedom of being able to start from scratch. The few mistakes I made—in not tooling evenly or getting the headcap of leather a bit too thick—never seemed as obvious as a repieced leather spine glommed onto a rebacking. I understood the idea of trying to repair the damage to the spine while trying to keep the original look of the book's cover, but practicing my techniques on books from Special Collections sometimes seemed unfair to the books.

That year in the Conservation Department, we had been working on a number of the collections that comprise Special

Collections. David Schoonover had been sending down major English authors that needed work. Besides Scott, we were working on books by noted authors such as Lewis Carroll, Jonathan Swift, Henry Fielding, Lord Byron, Elizabeth Barrett Browning, and Robert Southey. There were a number of volumes sent down from the Leigh Hunt Collection.

One jewel I had the pleasure of rebinding was *Huon de Bordeaux*, a small volume from this collection. James Henry Leigh Hunt is known primarily for his friendship with Keats and Shelley, although he was a prolific writer himself. The University of Iowa has a large collection of his works and ephemera (including locks of hair of Hunt and Keats) that was assembled in the 1950s by Luther A. Brewer from Cedar Rapids. A gift to the university, the Hunt Collection has its own vault within Special Collections. Fortunately, at the time Bill gave me this volume—which contained Hunt's signature on the flyleaf—I had no idea how valuable it was.

Huon measured five and one-quarter inches tall by three and one-half inches wide. It was covered in brown calf that, like other volumes bound in 1800, hadn't aged well. Both the boards were loose, and the gold tooling had rubbed off most of the spine titling and decoration. The leather also had large brown spots where it was deteriorating. Rather than doing a simple rebacking, Bill and I examined the covers and decided that it should be completely redone. This was in opposition to the conservation tenet I would later learn from other teachers: the original covers should be saved and reused if at all possible to keep intact the integrity of the book.

The volume had come to me in a three-sectioned wrapper of green book cloth over board that wound around the book to protect it. Then as a package it slid into a slipcase constructed with a deep green leather spine with raised bands and gold titling. The rest of the slipcase was covered in the same green shiny book cloth as the wrapper. With this construction, when the book was shelved, it appeared as if you were seeing the actual green leather spine of a finely bound book. I had no idea whether the protective enclosures had been made before or after the covers had come loose, but they undoubtedly had helped to keep the pieces together and in better shape than they might otherwise have been in. Bill also decided that I would make a new slipcase for the book when I was finished.

I removed the spine of the book, paring it off with my lifting knives. Since I didn't have to reuse it, I let the pieces of spine leather fall to the floor as they came off. Once I had cleaned off the leather and removed the paste and mull on the spine of the text block, Bill examined it again. He decided that the book was dirty enough to warrant full treatment, so I set about washing and deacidifying the pages and mending them before I reassembled the text block. For some reason I really liked this volume, although I confess to having not been a fan of Leigh Hunt's when I took the ill-fated class in which I had read William Blake.

I resewed the book over linen cords. That meant when I recovered the book, the spine leather would be shaped over functional cords on the spine, rather than over fake cardboard bands. The new cover was three-quarters leather, a wonderful vermilion calf with a complementary rust-and-peach marbled paper. And the blind and gold tooling I had been practicing on the leather rebindings went especially well on the spine.

I constructed a slipcase covered at the fore edge with a quarter inch of the same leather I had used on the binding. The rest of the slipcase was covered in a handmade paper that matched the tone of the leather. I was very proud of it when I finished it.

Bill selected it as one of the two of the pieces sent by the department and the University of Iowa Center for the Book to go on exhibit for four months at the Thomas J. Watson Library at the Metropolitan Museum of Art in New York as part of a show of books by students done at five schools in the country with book arts programs. I was thrilled that Bill thought it good enough to send to the exhibit. When the library was doing the paperwork to lend the book to the Watson, I discovered *Huon* was valued at more than $2,000. I was grateful no one had told me that earlier. It was the best of my leather rebinding and rebacking efforts that year, although I did get proficient enough to rebind eighteenth- and nineteenth-century books so that they didn't look as if beavers had been gnawing on the leather spines. Bill must have also noticed an improvement because in the next batch of books he gave me to do was my first incunabulum, *Historia Rerum Ubique Gestarum*, printed in 1477.

○ ○ ○

Book conservation program
receives Mellon grant

The University of Iowa Libraries have received a $140,000 grant from the Mellon Foundation for book conservation education.

The three-year grant will be used to support training of two apprentice conservators and for a series of seminars for professional book conservators.

The apprentices will train under William Anthony, University libraries book conservator. Anthony, a master bookbinder, has trained conservation apprentices for more than 20 years and is considered one of the top professional conservators in the country.

"University of Iowa Libraries are uniquely suited to offer book conservation training in that we have one of the finest book conservators in the country, William Anthony, to train these apprentices," said University Librarian Sheila D. Creth.

Apprentices will learn paper conservation relating to books from all periods, as well as the art of fine and rare binding, one of Anthony's specialties.

Advanced workshops funded by the grant will cover topics ranging from valuable pamphlet collections to nineteenth-century cloth case binding to non-adhesive versus adhesive book bindings on rare covered books. . . .

Anthony's apprentice conservators will benefit from the related book art programs of the UI Center for the Book.

—*fyi*, May 6, 1988

The Conservation Department and the library had received notification in late April of the Mellon Foundation's grant for workshops and apprentices. Bill made plans to teach the first workshop in October on conservation treatments of pamphlet collections. He went through Special Collections and brought a batch of pamphlets—mostly from the railroadiana collection—for me to work up as samples for the workshop students to study. The library administration prepared an advertising brochure and sent press releases to all the related conservation publications. Applications began to pour in, and Bill waded through them to pick out who would attend the first workshop.

The grant also covered the funding of two new apprentices to be taken on in the department. More notifications were sent out to the appropriate publications, and Bill weeded through those applicants as well.

At the same time, Bill resewed the constitution. As I worried over my own leather work, he rebacked the volume with new spine leather dyed to match the covers and built a drop-spine box to house it. Slides of the process were taken for the library's documentary, but media attention had faded. The narration for the documentary was being written by a work-study student in the department, Penny McKean, and Larry was busy binding the facsimile copy of the constitution. I was given the task of making the drop-spine box to house it, using a black-and-white tweed book cloth to match the brown-and-white tweed Bill had used for the original. It only took me two tries to get a box that wasn't too snug.

By mid-July, the constitution was finished and its new wooden case was being constructed. Deadlines eased up, and in June Bill took a group of us on a trip to Loras College in the northeast corner of Iowa to see their manuscript collection. Next we traveled southeast to Bloomington, Indiana, to see more book collections and the papermill at Twinrocker, one of the United States' foremost hand papermills. In July, Bill and I went to PBI, the annual two-week paper and book intensive workshop, held that year in a conference center in the wilds of Minnesota. It was great to get away to study and share with other teachers and book arts enthusiasts from all over the country. I especially enjoyed seeing Bill in a much more informal setting.

I vividly recall one evening before dinner, standing next to him on the deck just outside the dining room. Yells and laughter floated up to us from the volleyball courts below. We were drinking beer and leaning on the railing looking out into the trees that surrounded the conference center. Bill had on jeans and a plain T-shirt—very casual, indeed. It had been a long time since Bill and I had shared a beer. We chatted about how our workshops were going. I was taking a fabulous one on making pop-up books. I collected them and had always wanted to learn how to make them and I described the problems I was having with the carousel book construction I was trying to finish before the four-day session concluded. Bill was teaching a class on designing limited-edition bindings, and told me about the eight students in his classes and the problems they were having thinking about binding books in multiples. We agreed we were enjoying the break away from the library, and moved on to talk about his two new apprentices who had been chosen just before we'd left Iowa.

Bill wasn't sure what it would be like to guide four people at once and was worried about overstaffing the department. But one of the new apprentices, Sally, had worked in the department as a student for several years and already knew a lot about conservation and how the department ran. He hoped it would all go smoothly, that he would continue to have time for all of us, and that Larry and I would help the new apprentices settle in. I assured him that we would do whatever we could to help and that he would be able to manage just fine with four apprentices. The dinner bell sounded and we went inside to chicken casserole and fresh, warm blueberry pie. Bill looked relaxed and less tired than he had since all the fuss with the constitution had begun, and I enjoyed seeing him have a good time.

Shortly after we got back from PBI, Bill flew to California with his wife, Bernie. They were combining a vacation with Bill's filming a segment of an interactive video at the Getty Library on binding a twelfth-century, oak-covered book. After he finished several days' work on the video, he and Bernie traveled around California. One night, she took him to the emergency room because he was in terrible pain. The ER doctor told her that Bill needed to get home at once and see his own doctor.

On August 1, the day the two new apprentices began in
the Conservation Department, surgery revealed that Bill had
liver cancer. Except for two brief visits to see how we were
doing, he never came back to the Conservation Department.

○ ○ ○

*President Hunter R. Rawlings III and
The University of Iowa Libraries cordially invite you
to a special ceremony to mark the completion of
the restoration of the Iowa Constitution of 1857 and
its transmittal to the State of Iowa.*

*Monday, October 17 at 3:30 P.M.
Senate Chamber, Old Capitol
Iowa City, Iowa*

Reception immediately following.

It was a beautiful clear day in October. A Monday had been
chosen for the constitution ceremony because Bill had
chemotherapy on Thursdays and usually felt better by
Monday. Since this was such a public occasion, Bill wanted to
feel his best.

We had all worn dress-up clothes to work, and I found it
difficult to get anything done when I had to concentrate on
not getting my sweater sleeve in the glue bowl. I didn't
accomplish much. No one did.

We, the apprentices and student workers, all walked up to the Old Capitol before 2:00 P.M. to help set up. I stopped by a camera store uptown that was lending me a long-range lens to take photographs for the library. My macro lens, used for shooting pictures of books up close, wasn't going to be very helpful taking pictures of the ceremony in the Senate Chamber. I was sure that my flash wouldn't work and that I would take shot after shot of dark blobs.

By the time I caught up with everyone else, the second floor of the Old Capitol had been set up. One of the student workers had made a poster detailing the conservation treatment of the constitution, and it was resting on an easel next to a cart with a VCR and television that were set up to show the video of the slides documenting the conservation treatment. The constitution was laid out on one of the desks in the House Chamber, and at 3:00, University Librarian Sheila Creth, began to page through it slowly for the photographers who had arrived early. It was the star of the day.

Bill arrived just after 3:00 with Bernie and their daughter Lisa. We were all happy to see him able to attend this event, and each of us said a few words of greeting. As he stood under the glare of the television and photographers' lights talking to reporters, it was easy to see just how pale and thin he looked as a result of his illness and the chemotherapy. Months later, as Sally and I were looking again at some of the constitution slides taken from April through July, she said, "We should have noticed it. We should have seen how Bill was getting thinner and paler all summer." But we hadn't noticed.

Jon Van Allen, a photographer for the University of Iowa Foundation who had photographed Bill and his books on several occasions for the Center for the Book, was on hand for this important event. Shortly before the ceremony began, he grouped us, apprentices and students, around Bill for a photograph with the open constitution on a desk in front. Jon made each of us a copy of that photograph after Bill's death.

Just before 3:30, the dais was organized for the ceremony. Instead of taking his place next to Sheila Creth, Bill opted to sit in the front row of chairs between Lisa and Bernie. I stood in the back, next to Jon Van Allen, taking pictures. After all the months of preparation, the ceremony had a surreal feeling to it. After various speeches, President Hunter Rawlings presented the constitution to Secretary of State Elaine Baxter and Governor Terry Branstad. During the reception, Bill answered a few more questions from reporters and drank some punch while Sally and I took turns showing off the constitution. I could see Bill from where I stood behind the wooden railing in the House Chamber, slowly paging through the volume much as he had done all those months ago when it first came into his care. After an hour of all of these people and excitement, he looked wrung out. I tried not to think about it as I smiled and answered questions for the reporters. I don't think I'd had my picture taken that many times on my wedding day. The next afternoon, there I was, in color, on the back page of the front section of the *Cedar Rapids Gazette*, holding open the constitution.

In an interview that afternoon, Bill said, "We have done the work on the book. I consider the book to be probably the most valuable single document in the state. It belongs to all the people. And it was a great honor for us to work on such a document. Consequently, we went to extremes to make sure that the paper was in the best possible condition when it was restored." That afternoon, the constitution and its facsimile were driven home to the statehouse in Des Moines. It was the end of a long spring and summer for us all.

◌ ◌ ◌

BRANSTAD ACCEPTS RESTORED IOWA CONSTITUTION FROM UI

Following months of restoration at the UI Libraries Conservation Laboratory, the Iowa Constitution was returned to its rightful place.

UI President Hunter Rawlings returned the restored document, written in 1857, to Gov. Terry Branstad and Secretary of State Elaine Baxter at a ceremony in the Senate Chambers of the Old Capitol. The document was taken to the state capitol in Des Moines. . . .

UI Libraries Conservator William Anthony, an internationally-known conservator and book binder, headed the $10,000 project that began April 29th. . . .

Baxter said Anthony demonstrated true craftsmanship in restoring the 131-year-old document. . . .

"I think that all of the people of Iowa, the Governor and myself included, owe a great debt to you for allowing this document to survive for future Iowans," Baxter said.

"I can attest, as you all will today when you see this document, he has done excellent work," Baxter said. . . .

Rawlings said, . . . "Iowa and the UI are fortunate in having one of the finest resources in the restoration of documents."

—*Daily Iowan*, October 18, 1988

MASTERPIECE

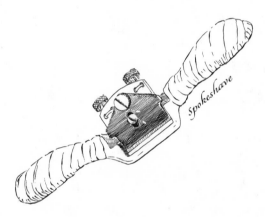

Spokeshave

At the end of my first year of apprenticeship, Bill had had his yearly review of the apprentices. Late one afternoon, he and I went into a corner of the break room and discussed how things had gone my first year. Bill told me that he was very pleased with my work. He said that he didn't know what kind of conservator I would end up being yet, but I would be wonderful at something. I was happy that he was satisfied with how I had been doing.

The one criticism he had was that I needed to concentrate more on my conservation training. I agreed with him. With my father's death and having to place my mother in a nursing home, plus graduate school and teaching rhetoric in the evenings fall and spring semester, I hadn't been focused enough on my apprenticeship. I was afraid to stop teaching because I wanted to be able to resume my teaching assistantship if the second year of my NEA grant didn't come through. But Bill assured me that the grant had been renewed, and he saw no problem with it continuing to be renewed throughout the rest of my apprenticeship—approximately five years.

After this review with Bill, I reconsidered graduate school. I had finished all my preliminary work for my Ph.D.

in English and was now working on writing my dissertation on the first English dictionaries. But after some thought, I had gone up to the registrar's office one day early that summer and had withdrawn from graduate school. I hadn't even told my husband, Scot, first. I wanted to focus totally on my work with Bill. And since he had just asked me to teach an intermediate binding class, I gave up teaching rhetoric as well. I got rid of as many distractions from my training as I could.

So in September 1988, I was ready to focus completely on my apprenticeship with no master to teach me. I prepared to teach a class I had never taught before without Bill's guidance. But instead, in his absence I was distracted and unfocused, as was the department as a whole.

○ ○ ○

Surveys done throughout the country indicate that as many as 25% of the books on library shelves are deteriorating. This is due to such factors as the acidity of their paper, inherent structural problems, storage conditions, and the wear and tear of use. Thus libraries are developing conservation and preservation programs to deal with the deteriorating books in their collections. The exhibit, *Saving Our Books and Words: The Conservation and Preservation of Books,* illustrates many of the methods of treatment now being employed at The University of Iowa Libraries on its most important collections. University Conservator William Anthony, with the assistance of his apprentices and student workers, has designed a step-by-step presentation of the work of the Conservation Department that should give viewers an insight into the complex problems of book conservation and preservation. The exhibit will be on display through mid-January.

—Invitation to the opening of *Saving Our Books and Words*

We found out that September that Bill, while working as part of the libraries' exhibition committee, had promised that the Conservation Department would mount an exhibition on the conservation and preservation of books in the North Lobby to be installed the first week of December. With Bill undergoing chemotherapy, it was up to the rest of us to prepare and install the exhibit in his place. We received from the exhibition committee a three-page document detailing the ideal timeline that should be followed for installing an exhibit in the North Lobby, starting nine months before installation. But we only had three months left to prepare our exhibit.

We had permission to go through the general circulation collection and find books to repair for the exhibit, so Sally and I spent one afternoon walking up and down, looking for sets of books that needed work. With suggestions from Bill, we planned to show the steps in typical cloth and leather rebackings, detail the conservation treatment of a pamphlet, include some information about the difference between conservation and restoration, and discuss some of the principles directing repairs in the library.

Larry took the two types of books we had chosen to work on to Bill to get his ideas about how to proceed. Bill was glad to have us visit one at a time, and we took turns going over to his house during his good afternoons. Sally and I were also working on gold tooling that fall, and it helped our progress to be able to take him our practice pieces to critique.

Sometimes Sally and I would drive over together. Bernie

would let us in and Bill would be waiting for us, sitting in his recliner in the living room. I would sit down on the sofa while Sally would perch next to him, sitting on the fireplace hearth, to show him her latest plaquette, a piece of book board covered with leather on one side and tooled like the cover of a book might be. Bill would examine the plaquette and make suggestions for Sally as to how to get her tooled lines more even or more completely filled in with the gold. I would sit on the sofa, watching them and looking out the sliding glass doors to the backyard where Bill's roses bloomed for the last time that season.

Then, when it was my turn, I would show him my tooling. I had constructed a dummy book structure by gluing together a number of pieces of board and shaping it with the convex spine of a book. Having glued leather onto the spine, I practiced lettering titles on the spine and would take Bill my latest efforts for his suggestions. Then I would take the dummy back to Conservation, peel off the old leather, attach new, and practice again. It helped Bill feel connected with what we were learning and doing, I think, and it certainly helped me to have that contact with him. I missed his instruction; but more, I missed his cheerful presence in the department, keeping me focused and motivated.

The exhibit helped draw the apprentices and students together and gave us something to do. Sally and Jane worked on the sequence of cloth rebacking according to a detailed plan that Sally had written out. Larry and I began working on the leather rebackings. I took slides of all the processes so that we could mount photographs for the exhibit for the stages of treatment—like washing and deacidifying—that couldn't be displayed.

I spent days standing on the department's stools, taking pictures of Sally's and Jane's hands as they performed treatments. I'm sure that this got to be very distracting for the others working around us, because it entailed my turning off a portion of the ceiling lights each time I took pictures so that I could shoot only with photo lights. With the help of the others, I spent afternoons and evenings writing descriptive labels of the processes we were going to show and the commentary we wanted to include in the exhibit. After much discussion, we'd come up with the title *Saving Our Books and Words: The Conservation and Preservation of Books.*

✧ ✧ ✧

Books have always been threatened. The earliest bookbinders quickly evolved methods of protecting the text by covering it with leather and wood, by wrapping the covering material all the way around the book and tying it up with thongs, by folding the covering material over the edges, by holding the covers together with clasps, by storing books in boxes. Even the medieval practice of chaining books to shelves or lecterns was a form of preservation.

As time has gone by, threats to the survival of books have become more and more serious. The materials that make up books almost from the beginning and especially since the invention of printing have gotten progressively worse. Rag paper replaced vellum, paper made from shorter fibers replaced rag paper. Alum sizing of paper—a process which allows the paper to be printed on—replaced gelatin sizing and, in the process, made the paper highly acidic. Pasted-on endbands replaced sewn-on endbands. Binder's board (a specialized cardboard) replaced wood for covers.

Accompanying the decline in materials was a similar decline in structure. Now the most common binding is the ironically named "perfect" binding. It is an economical method of binding that unfortunately does not stand up to heavy use or allow for repeated rebinding. Modern hardback books are seldom satisfactorily rounded and backed and consequently their text blocks pull away from the spine even as they stand on the shelf.

—*Saving Our Books and Words* exhibit label

We realized that the purpose of this exhibit was to educate library patrons (and probably some of the library staff as well) about what we did in our department—how we proceeded differently from the employees who repaired the general circulating collection. They were free to use nonarchival materials and techniques we were not and in a number of cases sent volumes off to be rebound in the standard library binding of the highly sized, shiny cloth hardcover we all associate with library books. When we had strolled though the stacks of the circulating collection looking for sets of books to work on for the exhibit, Sally and I had been surprised to see how much the differently treated volumes stood out from their shelf companions.

We would find attractive sets of leather- or cloth-bound books, such as the thirty-six volumes of *The Works of Rudyard Kipling*. This particular set was published by Charles Scribner's Sons between 1897 and 1937. With illustrations "by the author," the creamy pages have deckle edges and are sewn through the fold so that the volumes open easily. Each is covered in what originally was maroon cloth with gold titling and water lilies stamped on the spines. In the center of each front cover is an embossed medallion of an elephant's head, echoed on the title pages, that has been painted to form an ivory-colored disk. Glaring out from the shelves where these volumes of Kipling are housed are volumes that have been rebound in library bindings, such as number 20, the *Just So Stories*. The book was obviously often read by library patrons, and its cover must have broken down. It had been sent off to Gaylord, or one of the other library binding services, to be rebound in shiny maroon book cloth. It had been resewn, side-stabbed, the gutter margin so tight it was more difficult to open than its elephant-embossed brothers, and the edges of the pages had been trimmed of their deckle edges for neatness and uniformity in the new cover. Another volume in the series had been treated the same way, rebound in shiny brown book cloth.

To find sets of books like this shocked and annoyed me in a way it never did when I was just a graduate student looking for a source for my paper on T. S. Eliot. Certainly these volumes of Kipling are found on the shelves of numerous libraries across the country, but the integrity of *these* volumes as a complete set has been lost.

Of course, having worked in the library, I know the general collection needs more upkeep than an army of preservation librarians could afford to give it. The library couldn't afford the time it would take to restore the *Just So Stories* to better condition and more compatible appearance. Wandering among the stacks, Sally and I found many instances of cloth- and leather-bound books in sets that had been carefully rebacked with the original spines replaced. But in many instances, it was cheaper and quicker to send them off to be rebound. I understood, but these books made me want to scream.

These "library bindings," as they are called, are found in other more unsuitable places in the library as well. There are older, more valuable texts that were rebound in library bindings before being housed in Special Collections. In several instances, volumes several centuries old were cut and trimmed to fit into their shiny new covers. Occasionally, whoever rebound these in their new library bindings or ordered the rebinding realized that these were "old" books and took some trouble with the new binding. While looking for examples of books covered in different types of marbled paper for a class we were teaching in decorated papers, Sally and I found a Hebrew volume, printed in 1822, bound in new library binding, with fake, printed marbled paper as endsheets. Once the edges of the pages had been trimmed, they had also been marbled in a red swirl pattern to make the volume look even more elegant. This treatment was outlandish for a volume of the period, and I pleaded for this book to be cut loose from this manacle and rebound more appropriately.

Indeed, for a while the Conservation Department had an employee who would wander the stacks searching for volumes

that he considered to be old and valuable enough to be put in
Special Collections so they would no longer circulate and would
have better care taken of them. It was an altruistic quest, but
Special Collections simply couldn't handle that many new volumes. It was already strained for places to put acquisitions.

◌ ◌ ◌

The Conservation Department in the Main Library of The
University of Iowa was started July 1, 1984, under the direction
of William Anthony, University Conservator. Dale Bentz,
former University Librarian, and Kim Merker, Director of The
University of Iowa Center for the Book, were responsible for
bringing Anthony from Chicago where he had a private conservation studio.

In addition to conserving valuable books and documents in
the Library's Special Collections Department, the Conservation
Department is deeply committed to the training of apprentices
and interns. At this time there are four apprentices and two
interns in the department. The apprentices will undergo six
years of training before qualifying as book conservators. The
interns will eventually qualify as technicians or possibly replace
apprentices who have completed their training.

A special project of the department has been the develop-
ment of a unique collection of models that demonstrate the evo-
lution of the codex—the form of the book as we know it. This
collection has been exhibited in various museums throughout
the country, including the Art Institute of Chicago and the
Metropolitan Museum of Art in New York.

Anthony and two of his apprentices, Lawrence Yerkes and
Annie Tremmel Wilcox, teach bookbinding in the Saturday and
Evening Class Program.

—*Saving Our Books and Words* exhibit brochure

Even though I had been teaching for years, I was scared to take on the intermediate binding class. What did I know about showing people how to bind books? I was used to teaching reading, writing, or speaking in rhetoric classes. Teaching bookbinding seemed much more difficult to me. How could I teach people to do things well with their hands?

In my class, not only would I have to teach students how to make simple case bindings for hardcover books, I also would have to construct those bindings in front of them while doing my demonstrations. When teaching rhetoric, I have never had to sit down in front of my students and write an essay. I was extremely uncomfortable with this idea of showing my students my bindings as I did them. What would happen when I made a mistake?

After Bill had asked me to design and teach this new course, I had planned exactly what I would do. Since the students I would get would have all done the same six bindings in Larry's elementary class, I knew what background they would have. I made samples of the bindings they would do and practiced making them myself.

Since I had previously taught in the university's Saturday and Evening Program, I knew the director who interviewed me again when I was approved as an instructor through the Art Department. She was glad that I was going to be teaching one of these binding classes and expressed her concern that the binding classes weren't academic enough. There were no reading or writing assignments given to the students as there were in many of the other art classes. I knew that I couldn't change how the other two classes were taught, but I had been a rhetoric teacher too long to give up incorporating reading, writing, and speaking into a course I was teaching—no matter what its subject matter was.

As I prepared the outline for that first semester, I added readings about binding history that we would discuss occasionally. I wanted students to be able to place their bindings in a historical perspective. When *did* case-bound books arrive in the history of binding? This also allowed the students time to ask questions and examine and discuss the department's collection of historical bindings.

I was used to having students evaluate each other's speeches and essays, so I adapted that to have my students write self-evaluations of their bindings as we finished them. This helped them focus on the work they had done before we discussed completed projects as a group, and it also helped them vent their frustrations over what had gone wrong. Unlike a writing class where students might have several chances to draft an essay, the time students could work on a binding was limited to class time, when they had materials and equipment available. They only did each binding once, and whatever mistakes they made they had to live with. Things often went wrong for them. In our group critiques, students individually presented the binding they had completed, discussed their successes and failures, and described what they would do differently the next time. Other students offered comments as the books were passed around the group.

I also assigned a final essay for which students had to evaluate a book they owned on the basis of everything we had learned about book structure over the course of the semester. These were presented orally to the group on the last night of class, as they each showed their books to the group. Even the shyest student was comfortable with the class by then, and they always chose such intriguing books that this evening was especially interesting. Students critiqued their favorite wild, ugly, and awful books.

Because of my background in teaching, I felt comfortable adding these components to a "craft class." I always felt that the students profited from them. I also came to discover that these components helped the students who weren't "handy." In almost every class, it turned out there was one student, who, try as hard as he or she might, just couldn't get the hang of the binding techniques we were learning.

○ ○ ○

This exhibit, *Saving Our Books and Words: The Conservation and Preservation of Books*, demonstrates the step-by-step procedures conservators take to extend the life of books so that people can continue to experience them in their original form. These procedures include the very topical area of washing and deacidifying the paper, but also the more mundane and more difficult areas of disbinding and rebinding books in cloth and leather. The exhibit also gives examples of conservation bindings and protective enclosures. What the exhibit cannot do is show the years of benchwork which are necessary for conservators to

perfect their craft so that they can address all of the issues and
handle all of the materials necessary to restoring books to usable
shape in a form as much like the original as possible.

—*Saving Our Books and Words* exhibit brochure

The exhibit opened on Wednesday, December 7, 1988. Each
time an exhibit opens in the Main Library, there is usually a
speaker who gives a lecture on a related topic, followed by a
reception in the North Lobby, where the librarians who
installed the exhibit officially open it for other staff members
and invited Friends of the Library. Everyone mills about and
has hors d'oeuvres and punch. We had gotten Bonnie Jo
Cullison, preservation librarian and head of the Conservation
Department for the Newberry Library (and former student of
Bill's), to come from Chicago to give a talk, "Some Thoughts
on the Preservation of the Human Record."

I had designed a poster with an illustration of a cut-away
book. These had been enlarged, and I hand-colored one for
each entrance of the library. The illustration was duplicated on
the invitation and exhibit brochure covers. For us, this exhibit
was a tribute to Bill. In fact, it bordered on being a shrine.

Sally and I made detailed sketches of the exhibit cases in
the North Lobby. As we were installing the books, labels, and
enlarged and mounted photographs, Larry had the idea of
placing some of the tools we used when we performed treatments into the exhibit cases to show people what they looked
like. The exhibition committee's guideline had encouraged
us to find "artifacts" for the display cases "relevant to the

exhibition." All of us were busy using our tools, so we placed Bill's in the cases. His timeworn paring knife was placed next to the partially pared spine in the case detailing leather rebacking. One of his lifting knives sat next to the volume with its spine removed. I put his wooden-handled awl and needles next to the sewing frame displaying a partially sewn book. I added a spool of the department's Irish linen thread.

Bill came to the opening and to hear Bonnie Jo's talk. He arrived before she began and sat on the very end of one of the long, blue cushioned benches in the North Lobby. I sat down next to him. It was the last time I was ever alone with Bill. He had become a precious treasure, and everyone wanted to be with him. I'm sure it must have been exhausting for Bill to be around people who wanted so desperately to be with him. As I sat next to him he scanned the room, taking in all our months of hard work. He turned to me and said simply, "It's wonderful."

The exhibit was quite well received by the library community. There was some talk of it being packed up and sent around Iowa to other libraries—a sort of dog and pony show for book conservation. We were invited to install the exhibit early the next spring in the State Historical Society Building in Des Moines. But the library balked at having the items from Special Collections on display in less secure conditions, so the exhibit was trimmed to just the cloth and leather conservation treatments. Some of the other items were replaced; some were dropped entirely. By the time it went to Des

Moines the first week of March, the exhibit was dedicated to Bill's memory.

○ ○ ○

Bill died on Wednesday, February 8, 1989, with his wife and family around him.

Following so closely on the heels of the restoration of the state constitution, newspapers throughout the state printed Bill's picture and obituary. I cut them all out and pasted them in the scrapbook I kept about the department while I was an apprentice. Each obituary noted in some form: "Anthony is survived by his wife, Bernadette, four children, four grandchildren, one brother and two sisters." Although I fully realized that the brunt of this great loss was borne by Bill's family, I couldn't help but wish that each one of those obituaries had added to the list of those left behind: "and four apprentices."

I don't remember much about the day Bill died. I remember the phone call that came from his family telling us. Letting us know about the visitation, about the memorial service arrangements. I remember going with Sally to a florist and ordering an amazingly large and bright bouquet of flowers to be sent to the funeral home. I remember making a large container of spaghetti sauce and taking it to the house the next day for the family. I remember the silence of the visitation that evening. Former students and apprentices, having flown in from somewhere else, came through the big, double wooden doors and down the aisles to be hugged and greeted by Bernie in whispered tones. I remember the seemingly huge wooden casket with its carving of oak leaves, flanked by Bill's fine binding of the Book of Kells and the color photograph Jon Van Allen had taken of Bill's hands sewing the endband on a large book. From where I was sitting, halfway back in the memorial chapel, the light captured in the photograph seemed to make the hands glow. I sat and stared at them. Any second they would begin to move and finish sewing the headband. I remember desperately wanting to get out of that room and finally going out to gulp in the cold February air. I remember the memorial Mass at St. Thomas More's the next day and people speaking on and on, and finally the smile that came when former apprentice Bill Minter eulogized Bill as the "Johnny Appleseed of bookbinding." I remember the reception afterward: trays of food laid out on Irish linen tablecloths, one of them mine. I remember wishing it was all over and far in the past.

When it had become apparent that Bill was too ill to ever come back to work, the question for the library administration became what to do with us. The Mellon grant had guaranteed two new apprentices, yet we had no teacher for them. The library did its best to see what it could do to help us.

The administration took suggestions from us and brought in several conservators from other institutions to teach us for a week at a time. It was a wonderful idea that brought several former apprentices and students of Bill's into our midst. One of his former apprentices, David Brock, was scheduled to come for what turned out to be the week after Bill died.

I think we got through that week after the funeral because David was there to occupy our minds and our hands. We spent five days tooling leather spines, learning tricks and secrets— some of which Bill had taught him. Tooling demands constant attention and thought, so it was necessary to concentrate. It was a healing experience to have this person with us who, although very much an individual master craftsman, had some of Bill about him, such as the way he rocked forward to tool lines into the spine of a book. Or the careful way he evaluated what we'd done and made positive suggestions about what to try next. I think it helped us get through that week to have this kind and caring person to keep us occupied with lessons.

Many times over the next several months, I had occasion to talk to people I knew in conservation or binding who expressed their sorrow at our loss. For the most part, however, we were left on our own to try to deal with it. We received one letter of sympathy from our close friend, Tim Barrett, papermaker for the university's Center for the Book. The original was typed on a thin piece of his wonderful creamy flax paper. I kept a photocopy that retains the spirit of the original:

Dear Larry and All,

Not long after I returned from studying papermaking in Japan, I was somewhere in the Southwest, driving my van on a lecture tour, thinking and watching the road go by. I was contemplating papermaking, and what I wanted to accomplish during my life; meditating quietly to myself. Amidst the jumbled thoughts, rather suddenly and without warning, it occurred to me I would never be able to undertake what I wanted in my lifetime. I suddenly realized it was impossible and that, at 29 years of age, I was already out of time. It couldn't be done.

I was a little shocked, and frightened at first, and then I realized there was a way, and only one way to get it all in. I had to find a way to inspire others, people younger than I, to tackle what I would never be able to get to. If I could do that, I realized, after I was physically gone I would still be accomplishing what I set out to do through those who had worked under me and around me. When this became clear to me, I felt much more calm and comfortable, and much more ready for the notion of my own death.

Many years later, a year ago in October to be exact, I received word that the teacher who had inspired me most when I was in Japan had died of leukemia, at the age of 40. While I cried, and while I am happy and proud to say that I did, I was absolutely convinced that Katsu Tadahiko was not dead, but lived in all of us who cared about the same things he cared about.

Therefore, amidst the sorrow and the grief that we all feel, and in spite of all the tears that we all shed, I submit to you with great sincerity that Bill is not at all dead, but very truly alive in all of us. We have no obligation to grieve, but only to stand for the things he stood for, to carry on his person and his ideals in ourselves and in our work, to teach others what he taught us. If we do that, we will have him with us always, and so will many others who never met him.

I send you my love and affection. To the extent that it is possible, please try to be borne up by those of us around you. We are thinking of you and Bill, and we care for you all very deeply.

Sincerely,

Tim

It was the only expression of sympathy we received that made me feel like someone really understood the situation we were in.

○ ○ ○

Of all these threats to the survival of books, the one which has gotten the most attention is the problem of acidic paper. Popular magazines and newspapers as well as specialized journals have featured articles about the "brittle books" problem. That is:

acidic paper. This is almost universally considered *the* most critical problem facing library collections today. And indeed it probably is. At least for books published from the 1850s on. If a book's covers are coming off, it can be boxed or wrapped in paper until a binder can get to it; but if the paper is self-destructing, there is a limited time for finding a solution before the book turns to dust.

Solutions to all the book problems can be listed under the general headings of preservation and conservation. Simply defined, preservation is the attempt to save the intellectual content of books while conservation is the attempt to save both the intellectual content and its vehicle—the covers, paper, endbands, etc. The former is concerned with saving what the human record contains without regard to the forms it winds up in. The latter focuses on the artifact itself, attempts to save *this* book, *this* sheet.

Ideally, librarians would save everything they have exactly as it is. But when a book gets to a certain stage of brittleness—or more realistically, when tens of thousands reach this stage at the same time—little more can be done than microfilming their pages (or photocopying or republishing or entering the words on a computer disk), preserving content while tossing the old pages away.

Implicit in conservation, on the other hand, is the belief that the medium is part of the message—that a book which looks and feels and operates exactly like the original conveys something to the reader which the same thing in another format does not. It is safe to say that a person holding a copy of Walt Whitman's first edition of *Leaves of Grass*—an edition Whitman personally helped set the type for—experiences the poems differently than he would reading a microfilmed copy of it. Or that a person reading the first edition of *The Origin of Species* would have a different feeling for the context it came from than he would if he were reading a modern paperback edition.

—*Saving Our Books and Words* exhibit label

As I served my apprenticeship, I often considered why some volumes were put away in Special Collections, such as those editions of Walter Scott, while others were not. This came up during discussions while we prepared the books for the exhibit and worked out definitions of conservation and preservation. We went round and round about the difference between the two.

Conservation and preservation are terms that are commonly used almost interchangeably, but they have different meanings. The way that I finally came to distinguish between them was to think about preservation as the larger term, encompassing conservation as one of its elements. Preservation covers the whole program a library or similar institution undertakes to maintain its resources, including controlling temperature, lighting, and humidity, limiting access to vulnerable materials, and storing books on shelves that are not too crowded.

The University of Iowa Libraries haven't always excelled in these areas, although a preservation librarian was hired during my apprenticeship. It was often too hot in areas of the Main Library during the summer before the air conditioners were replaced, and Special Collections was equipped with a number of dehumidifiers that roared off and on as necessary. Before my apprenticeship was finished, I received firsthand experience in caring for water-damaged materials both in the library and the Art Building. And what library these days doesn't experience overcrowding on its shelves?

I also came to see during the course of working on the exhibit that preservation also means deciding what to do about a book that simply cannot be used any more: buy another copy, photocopy, or microfilm it? Preservation is primarily interested in saving the content of books, while conservation is intent on saving the artifact itself with as little change as possible to the physical object. Although I don't always think my treatments as an apprentice were as unobtrusive as they could have been, I did see the point in trying to keep conditions as close to the original for future readers.

But because of the nature of books, changing them is unavoidable during treatment. Even the beneficial step of deacidifying paper is a very invasive procedure because it radically changes the chemistry of the original. Add to that procedures such as resewing with new thread, covering books with new materials, and replacing broken or missing parts like headbands or covers, and book conservation begins to sound a lot like restoration. It *is* restoration, because unlike art such as sculpture, which is fairly static in its finished state, books have to function. They have to hold together and open. People have to be able to read them, not just look at them as some sort of soft sculpture.

There's a famous book artist, Philip Smith, who has done numerous fine bindings on Tolkien books. He does elaborate bindings in leather of scenes from this work. Then he takes a number of them and puts them together in big wall displays mounted behind Plexiglas to make more complicated landscapes where each book fits into the scene. Bill often used to express disgust about Smith's work when the name came up or pictures of these books were shown. "You can't read or handle books when they are mounted like that. What's the point of binding and displaying a text that way?"

The year before he got sick, Bill had taken us on a field trip to the Lilly Library in Bloomington, Indiana. There we saw a number of books that were bound in the French manner. The books were lovely to look at with their elaborate fine bindings in leather. But to open them fully would have broken the hinge area where it attaches the board to the spine. Bill admired the excellent leatherwork the French binders exhibited on their books, but was dismayed by how it restricted the opening of the books.

"What good is a book that you can't open?" I asked Bill, sitting across the table from me.

"Some people say it's no good at all," he replied. "Then it becomes an object, not a book to be read and reread." I was always able to open easily any book Bill bound. Beauty and design and function of the volume always went together for him.

Book conservation attempts to do as little as possible to the original to keep it functional. Conservation fits within the broad concept of preservation by trying to preserve the words of the past, and at the same time, save the vehicle that has carried the words to us.

○ ○ ○

Part of preservation is securing books in the exact state they happen to be in. Below is a limp-vellum bound book, *Vita del*

Cardinale Roberto Bellarmino, printed in Rome in 1624. It was decided that since this is a first edition and an unusual bookbinding structure, nothing should be done to alter it. Instead a drop-spine box was made to protect it while it was being shelved or being used.

—*Saving Our Books and Words* exhibit label

The summer before I taught my first bookbinding class for the Saturday and Evening Course Program, Bill and I had planned carefully what I would teach: three small hard-cover bindings (quarter-, half-, and full-cover cloth), a slipcase to house them, a flax-paper portfolio, and a rounded-spine book sewn on tapes. I planned week-by-week what we would do to finish everything neatly, on time, by the end of the semester. But the semester wouldn't stay that well organized.

I will forever see them in my mind, working at the benches in Conservation: Lisa, Andrew, Paul, Razad, Amy, and Katherine—the students in my first intermediate bookbinding class, fall 1988. The class met in the Conservation Department one evening a week. The students were enthusiastic. Very enthusiastic. Whatever I showed them, they fell to doing with an exuberance the department hadn't seen in quite some time. I devoured their energy and pushed them harder.

One of the first lectures I gave them was on how to watch someone teach them a craft. I tried to remember the hardest aspects of observing Bill from when I was a new apprentice. I told them to carefully watch what I was doing with my hands at all times, and to ask questions if I did something that I didn't explain. Razad was very good about this. An engineer and a calligrapher, he had an intuitive sense of mathematical proportions and how books should look and function.

One aspect of teaching a handcraft that I had difficulties with was explaining how to measure pieces of board and cloth and paper. I have always had a bad time with numbers, often misreading rulers and mismeasuring things in my early days as an apprentice. Bill had noticed this and taught me ways to measure parts for books and boxes so that I would never know what numerical measurements I was working with. Rather than using a ruler to see how wide a book was when measuring for a box, I took a strip of paper and simply ticked in pencil on it the width of the book. Then I transferred that measurement to board or cloth as necessary. I never knew that the volume was six and three-eighth inches wide.

Because this was the only way I was confident of taking measurements, I taught all these shortcuts to my students. I would find Razad staring at me, his head slightly tilted during my explanations. Then he would go back and whip out his shiny metal ruler and take precise measurements that almost always resulted in an accurate transformation into a book. I am sure he considered me measurement disabled. Sometimes I would catch him quietly reexplaining to another student in numerical terms something I had said. I always told my students to use whatever method of taking measurements worked for them.

Sometimes after I had set them to a task, I would go to my bench to work on my other projects from the daytime. At one point that semester, close to midterm, I was working on a drop-spine box. My students were fascinated by the one I was making and asked if they could learn to make one, too. Again, infused with their enthusiasm and without Bill to warn me that this was inappropriate material for an intermediate class, I agreed. We added boxmaking to the end of the syllabus. I had no idea how long it would take inexperienced students to make a drop-spine box. We went through finals and into the week before Christmas to get everyone's finished. I never let students talk me into changing my syllabus again.

Part of the problem was Katherine. A university employee by day, she was an aspiring book artist by night. She also was completely inept. Her intentions were good, but her measurements were always just a bit off, no matter how she took them. Her text blocks were always just a bit too big for her covers, the pages sticking out from the fore edge. She always managed to get glue where it shouldn't be, such as smeared across the front of her cover. She had a heart of gold and boundless enthusiasm for what I was teaching, but it took her twice as long as everyone else to do the work and something always went wrong along the way. In some ways, she reminded me of Nadine, the student who had been in the first two semesters of Bill's class with me and who had no common sense when it came to bookbinding. I knew Bill had found teaching her frustrating. But he and I had only discussed the bindings I would teach in intermediate, not the types of students I might get.

I came to discover that there was a student like this in my class almost every semester. They watched me do the same demonstrations that everyone else did, received the same instructions, but for some reason, they simply could not make their hands do the right things to get the bindings to come out correctly. Charmain, a last-semester senior, had taken elementary and intermediate bookbinding to get the final credits she needed for graduation. She had no intention of ever making books again. As a result, she didn't want to invest in the proper tools for the course. Instead of buying an X-Acto knife that was sharp enough and small enough to do the necessary tasks, Charmain insisted on using a carpet knife that she had found at home. In the course of trimming the covers for her full-, half-, and quarter-cloth bindings, she cut completely through the covers and had to start over three times. After the third time, I told her to get the correct knife or flunk the course. Such students kept me striving to instruct clearly and made teaching a challenge.

○ ○ ○

Books which have pages that are too brittle to be rebound are likely candidates for encapsulation. This involves taking the book apart, washing and deacidifying the sheets, trimming the sheets to individual leaves, and encapsulating each leaf between two sheets of clear Mylar. Encapsulation is achieved by ultrasonically welding the two sheets of Mylar together around the leaf. A little excess Mylar is left at the spine edge so that the encapsulated leaves can be side-sewn together and covered, allowing the end product to function as a book. The

> Conservation Department uses a Minter Ultrasonic Welder, a machine invented by William Minter, a former apprentice of William Anthony.
>
> Encapsulation is not lamination. The former is a completely reversible process while the latter is not. An encapsulated document can be easily retrieved by simply cutting through the weld, whereas a laminated document is permanently—and often tragically—glued to the plastic that surrounds it.
>
> —*Saving Our Books and Words* exhibit label

After Bill's death, I still hadn't finished all of the last set of books he had given me to work on. A number of them were the pamphlets that he had wanted me to prepare for the proposed Mellon workshop on pamphlet treatments. One of them, *Songs for the Grange*, had pages of a very soft paper. The back cover was missing and the front cover was very worn. Its pages were extremely acidic. After I washed and deacidified it, I decided that it was too fragile to be rebound, so I decided, with some consultation with Larry, that it needed to be encapsulated.

I had done a number of encapsulations at this point. *Gray's Atlas Map of Iowa. Topographic Map of Winneshiek County, Iowa.* All maps. *Map of the Saint Paul and Duluth Railroad.* All flat. *Sketch of the Public Surveys in Iowa Territory.* But of varying sizes. *A Township Map of the State of Iowa.* One of them, *Carte de l'Amérique Méridie*, had been cut into seventy-two, six-by-twelve-inch pieces, all mounted on strips of blue silk. The strips were joined into four large pieces, six inches by three feet.

When it came to my bench from the Map Collection, the

silk had broken down in many of the folds, leaving sections free. I stretched out the pieces across the floor and photographed it in the condition it had come to me. Like many of the other maps I had encapsulated, it was hand-colored and probably couldn't be washed or deacidified. A sample test with a cotton swab wet with distilled water showed that the hand colors were fugitive and would run if the map were submerged. Another wet swab test showed that the blue of the silk was also fugitive and would run if dampened from the back, one of the usual methods of softening the adhesive of a backing material. And it was too firmly adhered to peel off. Sometimes when maps are backed with fabric—a common mounting method—the glue dries and hardens to the stage where the fabric can simply be peeled off the back. This was not the case for *Carte de l'Amérique Méridie*. So the silk had to be removed using a "blotter sandwich."

A blotter sandwich is a contraption formed by trapping a piece of the silk-backed map between two pieces of Hollytex polyester webbing. Then that is layered between two pieces of damp blotter that are then sandwiched between two pressboards and left to rest. In the case of the map pieces, after about two hours, the moisture traveling through the Hollytex into the map and silk sufficiently softened the adhesive, allowing me to easily peel the silk from the back of the map without damaging it. Blotter sandwiches are an effective way to moisturize items that can't withstand direct application of water. It took several days of piles of pressboards sitting around dampening map pieces, but when I was through, all of the silk had been successfully removed.

I had labeled the pieces in pencil before beginning this process in a maplike grid of letters of the alphabet and numbers. The letters designated the rows horizontally; the numbers indicated the rows vertically. After the map pieces were dried between pressboards and dry blotters and Hollytex, I reassembled the entire map as it had been originally printed before being cut apart and mounted on the silk. I pieced it together with just enough strips of kozo to hold it intact. Then I encapsulated it to the full size of forty-seven by sixty-two inches. Now it was one large flat map that could be used. There was nothing to be weakened by folding—the greatest stress on any map—and the Mylar would protect it and help hold all the pieces in place. I laid it on the floor again, photographed it while standing on my stool, and then sent it back up to the Map Collection on the third floor. So all of my encapsulation work to date had been of two-dimensional items. *Songs for the Grange* presented a problem because it needed to keep its book form.

I asked Larry how to encapsulate pages for binding. I knew that there was some trick involved in having the pages thick enough in the spine area to accommodate being bound, yet thin enough in the hinge area to be flexible for binding. Larry had a few general comments—he had done one or two such bindings—but it had been a long time ago, and he had no written notes of the process. Sally as well had completed several encapsulated books while a student worker in the department. Bill's daughter Lisa, who had done a lot of the single-page encapsulation for the Dada volumes Bill had encapsulated when he first came to the university, was no longer around to give me any hints. I was stuck. I had a book to encapsulate and no one to give me any clear directions on how to bind it.

I contemplated this problem for several days. Finally it occurred to me that I didn't have Bill in person anymore, but I had numerous samples of his encapsulated bindings. I went upstairs to Special Collections to see David Schoonover.

"I'd like to see books that Bill encapsulated," I told him.

"Do you have any titles?" he asked.

"No."

He considered this for a moment and then led me back into the locked stacks. We wandered around for a few minutes until he came to rest in the aisles of the Dada collection.

"Bill encapsulated a number of these early on. It was one of the first collections to receive treatment. Perhaps what you want is here."

I thanked him and sat down on the floor, pulling books off the shelves that showed the unmistakable spines of encapsulation: straight and flat like the back of a box, covered in library book cloth with hand-stamped labels. I looked at the dates on the treatment cards pasted to the inside of the back covers and tracked the dates to pick out those that would have fit the time frame David described: 1984–85, when Bill first began as University Conservator. Some of the books had pages that fanned open more easily than others. I finally collected those and took them out to a table in the reading room where I had left my pencil and pad.

I spent quite some time poring over the books, looking carefully at the page constructions to see how they were set into the spine. I came to distinguish the ones Bill had done himself because they opened well and were immaculately executed. Two hours later I went downstairs and began to encapsulate *Songs for the Grange*. My first attempt at encapsulating a book didn't open as well as the ones in Special Collections that Bill had done. I tried to figure out what had gone wrong and then returned to look at Bill's books again. My next attempt did open as well as one of his. I had discovered one new way to teach myself a new technique. I had to fine-tune my powers of observation even more.

○ ○ ○

These are the pages of a Russian pamphlet printed in 1923 on paper much like newsprint. Its pH was 3.5, which necessitated it being washed and deacidified. That changed its pH to 8, but the pages were still so brittle, they could barely be handled. The decision was made to encapsulate it. The pages were cut apart and sealed together between sheets of Mylar as shown below. They are now ready to be bound together in a single volume.

Two basic goals are achieved through encapsulation: retaining the book form and protecting the paper. Once the pages have been encapsulated they can be handled with no further damage to the paper. This example shows a book completely encapsulated.

—*Saving Our Books and Words* exhibit label

I slowly worked my way through the last books Bill gave me to do. I did more maps from the Map Collection. But I still had the *Historia*, the incunabulum. It became personified, sitting on my bench, watching me do other things. It was the oldest book Bill had given me to work on. It sat and waited. And sat and waited. I kept putting it off.

The library administration knew that apprentices without teachers weren't learning many new things. It brought in three different conservators to work with us one week at a time. That was helpful. It would be an infusion of teaching that gave us new things to practice and try for a while. But then gradually the inspiration wore off and it was back to the same old books. I moped and cried at home, and I wasn't terribly productive in the library. We were interviewing for a new conservator to head the department. It would be exciting to have a new teacher, but I would never be apprenticed to that person the way I had been apprenticed to Bill. That new person would simply receive the four of us as part of the equipment in the lab. We all knew that. He or she would have to work with us in some way until we finished, and then pick his or her own new apprentices. My apprenticeship was over, and it was depressing.

I finally came through the wall preventing me from dealing with all this the May after Bill died. While watching David Brock teach us tooling, it had dawned on me that although it meant a great deal to have someone show me *how* to tool on leather, it was really up to me to teach myself. I decided that May that I would be apprentice to myself. If I didn't know how to do something, I would find out. We certainly had access to a wealth of binding and conservation information with the Guild of Book Workers library now housed in Special Collections.

I pulled the *Historia* toward me and began to fill out a survey sheet on its condition.

◌ ◌ ◌

The field of book conservation was virtually born in the 1966 flood in Florence, Italy. Bookbinders had been interested in the care of books before then—and some of the old classics of the field are still consulted—but with the 1966 flood and the growing awareness of the problem of acidic paper, the literature of conservation and preservation has increased exponentially.

—*Saving Our Books and Words* exhibit label

The *Historia* was a full-leather binding of mottled sheepskin. It had been printed in Venice in 1477. It had been rebound at some point into this cover with its nonpareil French marbled paper endsheets. The text block had been trimmed and the edges colored red. Inside the volume, white spaces had been left for scribes to add illuminated initial letters by hand— often done so that the first printed books resembled their superior predecessors, manuscripts. Small printed letters indicated which large capital letters were to have been but never had been.

The binding was in fairly stable condition. The boards of the covers were warped slightly outward to give the book a wedge shape. The first thing I had done for this book months before in September 1988 was to make it a protective enclosure, a clam-shell box with a flap that came over across the book to gently press out the bow in the covers. It had sat on my bench so long that when I came back to work on it, the covers were flat. I had to discard that now too large box and make a new one.

The cover had broken down in the hinge area of the spine at the head, the first place that books, no matter how they are bound, break down. When they are shelved vertically, this is where the stress is when the books are pulled off the shelves. If not taken care of, eventually the leather will be weakened all along the hinges as the stress transmits downward and the boards will come free. I needed to do a partial rebacking of the book. Rather than inserting new leather entirely over the whole spine of the book and reattaching the covers and the original spine piece, I was just going to slip in a new piece of leather at the top. It was very tricky to do since the boards and the spine piece would be in the way the entire time. Not only was I daunted by the task, I was stymied by the fact that I didn't have anyone to show me how to do this. So I did what still came naturally to me as a student: I looked it up.

It was not difficult to find instructions. I looked almost immediately in Bernard Middleton's *The Restoration of Leather Bindings*, in which a section of a chapter was devoted to partial leather rebackings. I was in good hands with Middleton.

An English binder, Middleton wrote the standard text on

the history of English binding, *A History of English Craft Bookbinding Technique*. It recounted in detail how English books had been constructed and decorated and produced throughout history. It was one of the first books I bought for my own binding library. *Restoration* not only had detailed written instructions of what I needed to do, it also had sketches and photographs of Middleton's long fingers to help guide me.

Whenever we had cause to refer to one of Middleton's books in the shop and Bill noticed, he would regale us with stories of this master craftsman. One of his favorite stories was about how Middleton once rebound an older book in a new cover. To get the new cover appropriately distressed and aged, he had carried it everywhere he went for several weeks—in a large leather attaché case with dirt in it! Bill always tried to make his new covers look appropriate to their time period, but he never went as far as that. But it was a story I remembered. Once when I needed to add new endsheets to a sixteenth-century text whose pages were still stained and dirty after washing, I dampened them slightly and wiped up the back counter of the department with them. That colored them randomly and sufficiently so that their newness wasn't apparent.

It was certainly more difficult to follow the instructions from Middleton's book that it would have been to ask Bill. I finally devised a way to prop *Restoration* up on my bench, and I completed the partial leather rebacking while following the steps out of the book, adapting them to the volume at hand. It was awkward, cumbersome, and very slow. Middleton didn't answer all my questions about technique, and I had to make several attempts to get the leather pared thin enough in the right places so that the new headcap looked and worked correctly when I readhered the spine piece.

I finally finished the last book Bill had given me to do on December 20, 1989, fifteen months after I had first started it. I was extremely proud to finish that last book, but it signaled for me the end of my apprenticeship. Although it was not necessarily my finest work, it was my masterpiece.

I guessed the book was not in its original binding, but *Historia* still had the patina of centuries of use. The mottled brown leather, cool to my fingertips, glowed through its bumps and rough spots. The spine with its few nicks and scratches still shone brightly with its gold tooled decorations and lettering. At the very head of the spine, my newly inserted leather matched almost perfectly the color of the original leather. The red edge-coloring of the text block burned out from between the covers.

I paged through the volume, wondering what the illuminated initials would have looked like had they been in place, admiring the soft feel of the paper, its imbedded texture mirroring the nap of the original wool felts the text paper had been pressed between. Made by hand in a century that put no harmful additives in its paper, the pages were as creamy white as the day they had been printed. The finely combed marbled endpapers had a high gloss from being burnished, yet they were casually irregular in pattern. *Historia Rerum Ubique*

Gestarum was not a deluxe edition, but it had great integrity. I shut the book and put it in its box.

○ ○ ○

The book has now been completely restored and is fully functional. Deterioration has been arrested and the book has been stabilized and repaired in a manner both structurally sound and completely compatible with its original form.

—*Saving Our Books and Words* exhibit label

Annie Tremmel Wilcox earned her Ph.D. in English at the University of Iowa in 1994. She has taught writing for more than fifteen years and presently teaches writing by correspondence through the University of Iowa. She also works privately as a rare book and paper conservator and teaches book arts. She is working on a second book, a collection of essays about food and family. She lives in North Liberty, Iowa, with her husband, Scot, and their children, Zachary and Emily.